ARC OF INTERACTION

Joseph A. Steger Student Life Center • University of Cincinnati

ARC OF INTERACTION
MOORE RUBLE YUDELL WITH GLASERWORKS

Edited by Oscar Riera Ojeda • Essays by Steven Litt and Ron Kull
Primary photography by Alan Karchmer

ORO *editions*

CONTENTS

THE JOSEPH A. STEGER STUDENT LIFE CENTER AT THE UNIVERSITY OF CINCINNATI
by Steven Litt

Colleges and universities once defined their rivalries in terms of sports and academics. Now they're scrimmaging over architecture and planning. To impress prospective students, and their parents, academic institutions are deploying architects, landscape architects, and campus planners to create new buildings and public spaces aimed at attracting and retaining the best and brightest. The new ethos has sparked extensive expansions and renovations across the country, with everything from chic new dormitories to lively new "college town" retail districts at the campus edge. Few institutions, however, have undergone as dramatic a physical transformation in recent years as the University of Cincinnati.

Under former president Joseph A. Steger, vice president Dale McGirr, and campus architect Ron Kull, the university launched an ambitious makeover in the late 1980s. Once a dowdy commuter school catering mostly to a local population, the university is now famous for having built one of the most important collections of contemporary architecture in the world—an astonishing fact, given the conservative cultural and political personality of Cincinnati. After establishing a master plan in 1991 designed by the leading American landscape architect George Hargreaves, the university spent more than $1 billion erecting important buildings by leading contemporary architects, including Frank Gehry, Peter Eisenman, and Michael Graves.

In the process, however, administrators discovered that iconic architectural statements only go so far when it comes to creating a sense of place. They learned that buildings in specific settings on a university campus should be designed to impart liveliness to the outdoor spaces around them—not to merely stand apart and strike a pose like fashion models on a catwalk. In other words, the university discovered the importance of urbanity.

The Joseph A. Steger Student Life Center, one of the more outstanding products of the university's physical renaissance, is a direct outgrowth of such understandings. Designed by Moore Ruble Yudell and named appropriately for the university president who led the first decade of Cincinnati's architectural revival, the building plays multiple roles as an eye-catching landmark, as a source of around-the-clock activity, and as a supportive backdrop to the lively social spaces around it. In many ways, it is a culminating statement of the university's architectural renaissance.

Shaped in plan like a slender, 550-foot-long parenthesis with sharp prows at the ends, the eight-level building houses heavily trafficked offices for student organizations, the university's co-op program, an art gallery, coffee shop, and other amenities. The building steps down as it curves from west to east to follow a fifty-foot drop in elevation along its length. Above a first story trimmed in brick to echo the older buildings on campus, the Steger Center sports façades of medium-gray zinc panels, with ribbon windows and triangular bay windows, which break the building's curve to grab lateral views for the corridor and offices above. A ground-level arcaded walkway edges the convex south side of the building, creating sheltered entries for the retail spaces within.

Taken on its own, the building is a dramatic object, somewhat reminiscent of a ship steaming through the heart of campus. The nautical analogy is made perhaps even more explicit through details such as a sixth-floor outdoor terrace, set on the building's east prow, where it overlooks a long vista across campus like a bridge near the bow of a ship. Then, too, the building is so narrow, at forty-two feet in width, that light penetrates the interior from both sides, like the cabin of a large vessel at sea.

Despite these suggestions of movement and flow, the Steger Center is firmly rooted in its setting. In fact, it is so intimately connected to its context that it's impossible to imagine it being built anywhere else. Along with two other buildings, it forms part of the university's new Main Street complex, conceived as a new, on-campus downtown for the university. The Steger Center turns its broad southern façade toward Bearcat Plaza, a roughly triangular outdoor piazza conceived by Hargreaves and campus planners as the heart of the complex. The plaza is edged on the southwest by the $51 million Tangeman University Center, designed by Charles Gwathmey, and on the east by the $101 million Campus Recreation Center,

designed by Thom Mayne of Morphosis. The plaza, in turn, acts as a central node along the university's half-mile "Campus Braid," a meandering pathway designed by Hargreaves to act as a thread unifying the university's once chaotic West Campus.

The university's decision to design and build three buildings around a new public space as a unified ensemble created a rare opportunity for the coordination of architecture, urban design, and landscape architecture. From the beginning, however, the university felt that the goal was not to orchestrate opportunities for contemporary architects to create a series of competing iconic statements. Instead, the goal was to have the architecture support the notion that the central space—the plaza—was the key focal point.

"The buildings are contemporary, but we didn't want them to scream and pound their chests," says Ron Kull, the university's campus architect.

The finished complex achieves a dense and lively atmosphere, something like that of an Italian hill town, where narrow alleys and pathways converge on a piazza framed by a cathedral, a city hall, and storefronts set behind arcaded walks. At Bearcat Plaza, the spatial drama was heightened by the university's brilliant decision to remove a series of brick concession stands on the southeast side of the space. The stands had blocked views into Nippert Stadium, the university's football field, which is jammed into a low-lying hollow just downhill from the plaza. Their removal opened a commanding view of the playing field below and turned the plaza into a belvedere.

Within this ensemble, the Steger Center plays a privileged role as the building whose mission is to provide a long, lively, pedestrian-oriented edge along the north side of the plaza. The other two buildings in the complex are internally oriented in their personalities, which means they don't play as important a role in activating the outdoor space.

The Campus Recreation Center, for example, edges the east side of the plaza with an outward-leaning, convex membrane of glass and metal, which seems to zoom through space at high velocity. It encourages students to do the same as they hurry from class to class. Inside, the Recreation Center houses a large gymnasium, a field house, an aquatics center, a student dormitory, classrooms, a climbing wall, and cafeterias with terraces overlooking Nippert Stadium. But few of these functions are made visible from the plaza.

At Tangeman University Center, which borders the southwest side of the plaza, Gwathmey hollowed out the core of a 1940s Georgian building to create a vast, soaring interior lobby and informal lounge. To incorporate an 800-seat auditorium, a large bookstore, and other facilities, Gwathmey wrapped the original building on three sides in a large, circular envelope, clad in a curtain wall grid of glass and

broad expanses of zinc panels. Tangeman University Center turns one of these curved sections toward Bearcat Plaza, where the effect, like that of the Recreation Center, is to send the eye flying through the space. This sends a signal that the plaza is a place to zip through, not a place to linger.

The Steger Center, however, does the opposite. It's designed to encourage hanging out, daydreaming, shopping, eating, and people-watching. Its ground-level arcade shelters storefront entrances for a Starbucks, a Subway sandwich shop, an art gallery, and a computer-supply store. The porous nature of the building guarantees lots of comings and goings along its entire length, with multiple opportunities for casual encounters. To further reinforce the building's conviviality, Hargreaves designed a series of curving, terraced seat-walls, ramps, and staircases, which all closely hug the curve of the façade. These forms simultaneously guide the flow of pedestrian traffic past the building and provide ideal places to stop and sit, soak in the sun, eat a take-out sandwich, and observe people as they traverse the plaza. The effect is somewhat like bleacher seats at a sports arena, a fitting analogy considering that from the seat walls on the south side of the Steger Center, one can see directly into Nippert Stadium on the opposite side of the plaza.

On its north side, the Steger Center takes on an entirely different personality. Here, the building presses close to the neoclassical buildings of the university's Engineering Quadrangle, which lies immediately to the north. Moore Ruble Yudell and Hargreaves turned the space in between into a long, narrow, terraced Mews Gardens, a canyon-like space with the character of a cloister. The Mews, which is cozy, intimate, and tranquil in comparison to the hustle and bustle of Bearcat Plaza, is divided into a series of intimate seating areas with tables and chairs edged by large, rectangular concrete planters filled with lavish greenery. Popular during the spring and fall, the Mews is especially sought after during the university's summer quarter, when competition for tables and chairs in the shade can be intense.

Sandra McGlasson, a professor in the Division of Professional Practice (the university's co-op program, which is housed in the Steger Center), says she has learned that "if you want to get a table" in the Mews, "you've got to get there early. During the summer, people fight for places there because it's so cool."

The two major outdoor spaces—the Mews Gardens and the plaza—are connected by a two-story portal, which bisects the waist of the Steger Center like a grand archway. When approached from either direction, north or south, the opening frames long, axial vistas of the buildings and spaces beyond, creating a sense of orientation and a sense of compression and release as strollers pass through the opening. "One could literally walk forty-two feet from a soft, intimate, episodic series of spaces (on the north side of the building) and experience a hard, fast, fluid, very vibrant space," says Mario Violich, a principal of Moore Ruble Yudell, who co-designed the building. "It's quite fascinating to see those parallel universes juxtaposed so closely."

The inseparable link between the building and the spaces around it creates a powerful, symbiotic relationship in which distinctions between architecture and landscape almost begin to blur. It's as if the building were an element of the Hargreaves landscape and vice versa. Yet it would be wrong to regard the Steger Center as a retiring presence. Viewed from its prow ends at the east and west, in fact, it seems to elbow a space for itself amid neighboring buildings like a dreadnought plowing through gaps in a crowded fleet. The west prow, in particular, seems to hurl forward with a racy, knife-edged blade of metal and glass, surmounted on the north side with a translucent, pleated canopy. The canopy shelters an outdoor stairwell and walkways that connect the Steger Center to renovated classrooms in Swift Hall, a neo-Georgian building in the Engineering Quadrangle just to the north. It's a powerful, unforgettable image.

Such adroit shifts in personality are the sign of an unusual sensitivity to context, which makes the Steger Center an example for campuses everywhere—if not for urban downtowns in general—of how an individual building can enhance social liveliness and create a sense of place while exploiting the opportunity, when appropriate, to strike a dynamic "look at me" pose. The building's accomplishments are all the more impressive for having cost a relatively modest $185 a square foot to construct—a price that means the university got a lot of architecture for its money. This makes it no surprise that the building was one of 11 to win a prestigious Honor Award as one of the best buildings of 2006 from the American Institute of Architects. In addition, the AIA Committee on Architecture for Education praised the building as "a vital insertion into the heart of the campus which reflects an interactive design process and speaks to the importance of the social aspects of learning."

To grasp the forces that led to the building's creation, it's important to understand the recent history of the university. Founded in 1870 as a city-owned institution, it grew steadily and haphazardly atop rolling hills about a mile-and-a-half north of the city's downtown and the Ohio River. By the late 1980s, the university had become a notoriously off-putting place. It consisted of two parts, a 57-acre medical campus and a 137-acre main, or West Campus, separated by some of the busiest boulevards in the city.

While the medical campus became crowded with hospital and research buildings and multi-story parking garages, the West Campus was packed with competent but unexciting Georgian-revival classroom buildings, rows of neo-Corbusian dormitory slabs, a football stadium, and the occasional Brutalist concrete research tower. A vast surface parking lot dominated the heart of the West Campus, providing a stark reminder that the university functioned primarily as a commuter school for local students who lived at home or in surrounding neighborhoods, who ate fast-food meals in their cars between classes, and otherwise spent as little time there as they could.

Steger, who became president of the university in 1984, saw the university's ugliness not merely as an aesthetic liability, but as a threat to its long-term survival. How could it attract and retain the best and brightest students and faculty, much less grow, unless it improved its physical setting? How could the University of Cincinnati compete with other colleges and universities that were luring students with lavish on-campus amenities and off-campus "college town" districts flush with retail, restaurants, and housing?

Within five years, Steger launched a new master plan, authored by Hargreaves, which called for the judicious demolition of outmoded buildings and a vast program of landscaping and new construction on both halves of the university. On the West Campus, Hargreaves replaced the vast central parking lot with a five-acre Campus Green defined by sculpted, wedge-shaped berms and the meandering Campus Braid. At the main entrance to the West Campus, Hargreaves placed a large conical mound covered with ivy, inspired by the prehistoric earthworks left behind by the indigenous peoples of southern Ohio. Students and visitors could ascend a spiral ramp to the summit of the mound and take in a panoramic view of the new educational terrain taking shape around them.

By 2001, both halves of the university possessed not only a series of stunning landscapes, but important contemporary buildings such as the Engineering Research Center, by Michael Graves (1992); the Aronoff Center for Design and Art, by Peter Eisenman (1996); the College Conservatory of Music, by Henry Ives Cobb (1999); and the Vontz Center for Molecular Studies, by Frank Gehry (2000). These and other buildings attracted global attention and inspired a guidebook published by Princeton Architectural Press. But by the early 2000s, administrators recognized that the University of Cincinnati, though it had come a long way, was still a collection of decentralized academic fiefdoms, each proclaiming its own identity through a photogenic building worthy of appearing on a postcard. They also realized they hadn't done enough to animate the outdoor spaces designed so painstakingly by Hargreaves.

"The (new) academic facilities were fascinating to look at, but they didn't express the idea that life was occurring on campus," says Thomas Hadley, associate vice president of Student Affairs and Services. "People disappeared inside the buildings. We wanted to create an environment in which people could sense life and vitality around them."

It is within this context that plans for the Steger Center evolved, in a series of creative leaps. The first and most important step was the simple realization that the university needed the building in the first place. The original Hargreaves Master Plan, dated 1991, doesn't include the footprint of the Steger Center. Nor does the architectural guide published by Princeton a decade later. By the early 2000s, however, university planners had quietly come to the conclusion that the proposed Main Street complex would require not two, but three new buildings. Kull, the campus architect, asserts that administrators discovered that they had about 80,000 square feet of program space that wouldn't fit either in the

renovated Tangeman University Center or the Campus Recreation Center. Those spaces—including student-government offices and services—had to go somewhere.

Students played a big role in the decision. In focus groups and meetings with individuals, university planners learned that students wanted easy access to services and to student-government offices, virtually at all hours, in a safe, transparent, highly visible setting. They didn't want the offices buried deep within large buildings, where they'd be invisible from public spaces outside. "Students really drove the design process" for the Steger Center, according to Hadley.

Hargreaves eventually proposed housing the student-government offices in a third building in the Main Street complex, located on the north side of Bearcat Plaza. But he suggested that the long, thin structure be laminated directly onto the southern façades of existing buildings in the university's Engineering Quadrangle. The university turned initially to the Cincinnati firm of glaserworks to act as executive architect. In turn, glaserworks recommended Moore Ruble Yudell as the design architect for the building. The firm's belief in the power of architecture to foster human interaction, detailed in the recent book, *Campus & Community*, caught the eye of Cincinnati administrators.

As the design process began, Steger remained highly skeptical that there was enough space on the north side of Bearcat Plaza to accommodate a third Main Street building. Violich, who co-designed the building, along with partner Buzz Yudell, also had doubts. He remembers thinking during an early visit to the campus, "There is no way this residual space can accommodate the Student Center." A large mechanical addition on the south side of Swift Hall thrust deep into the area where the Steger Center would have to fit. So did a cluster of mature trees and a series of buried tanks, which stored large quantities of gases used by laboratories in Rhodes Hall, one of the buildings in the Engineering Quadrangle.

Violich and Yudell became convinced, however, that it would be far more dramatic to pull their building away from those in the Engineering Quadrangle, but only slightly, to create the space for the long, narrow Mews Gardens. They discovered that if they could remove the Swift Hall addition and the nearby trees, their "sliver building" would fit through the narrow pinch point between the site for the Campus Recreation Center, to the south, and the Brutalist concrete massif formed by Rhodes Hall, to the north. The gap between their building and the flanking structures on either side turned out to be about thirty feet—just enough to accommodate emergency vehicles and pedestrian paths on the Campus Braid, and to avoid the buried tanks and utilities lines between the Steger Center and Rhodes Hall.

The result is a building that surprised everyone involved. "We had a gnawing sense that it wasn't going to work," Yudell says. "It took a leap on our part, and a leap of faith on the part of the university. The solutions we discovered ended up being varied and surprising because they weren't obvious."

Having proven that their building would fit surgically within its tight location, Violich and Yudell proceeded to give it a fine-grained sense of detail that seems to have grown out of the hard-won battle to make it fit in its site. Throughout the building, the architects rendered visible the steel-reinforced concrete framework that provides the building's structure, to communicate a sense of honesty and bare-boned elegance. Yudell described the brickwork on the lower level of the building's façades as an effort to link the building visually to older, classically inspired buildings on campus and to root the structure firmly in the earth. The zinc skin on the building's upper levels is intended, on the other hand, to link the structure to the two other buildings in the Main Street complex and, to an extent, to reflect the changing moods of the Cincinnati sky.

Light, flexible, and pliant-looking, the zinc façades communicate a rambling and relaxed informality that contrasts with the more systematic and formal façades of the other two Main Street buildings. The skin also appears to be tightly stretched over the building's underlying frame, like the exteriors of early twentieth-century Shingle Style mansions. At a finer level of detail, the zinc panels are affixed with vertical joints that create a syncopated pattern, further underscoring that this building is not governed by a rigid system but is, instead, a place to relax and enjoy informal contacts with fellow students.

The building's circulation system reinforces its conviviality. Yudell says the decision to place the glassy, single-loaded corridors on the south side of the building came from a conscious effort to echo the arcaded walk on the building's ground level on the structure's upper floors. "Early on, we decided on a single-loaded building, so the circulation in the upper levels would recapitulate the movement that happens along the passage at ground level. It's a signal of occupation and presence and community. Essentially, you're creating a series of streets on the upper levels so every student organization can have a front door and a reception area on that street."

On the building's southern façade, a series of horizontal, latticed canopies provide shade for the single-loaded corridors on that side of the building, while also creating a subtle sense of connection between the interior and exterior. The canopies gesture toward the students in Bearcat Plaza below, like hands waving from the windows. Such details hardly shout, but they're palpable nonetheless, and they give the structure a sense of care and follow-through that are crucial to any good building.

The building's narrow form and copious use of windows on both its northern and southern façades create the obvious benefit of flooding the interiors with daylight. The architects have calculated that over eighty-three percent of all occupied spaces in the building receive natural light, and that nearly all of the interior spaces have exterior views. Such factors were decisive in helping the building win certification from the U.S. Green Building Council's Leadership in Energy and Environmental Design program, or LEED®. As a building designed in 2000, the Steger Center was part of an early crop of projects to participate in the program, now a widely used standard in determining the environmental sensitivity of a building. Under the program, independent experts rate the performance of a building according to how well it conserves energy, and uses recycled and locally manufactured materials.

Users of the building report being delighted by the sense of connection to the outdoor spaces around the building, and by the ample penetration of daylight inside, made possible by the building's narrow width. "All of us have been transformed by the light," says Professor McGlasson, of the Division of Professional Practice. Some students have complained about the difficulty of traversing the building from end to end, a journey that requires climbing stairwells to get up and over the two-story portal carved amidships through the building to connect the Mews Gardens with Bearcat Plaza. But Michael Maltinsky of glaserworks, a member of the team that worked on the building, points out that the building's design exploits level changes to create dramatic vistas. A stairwell landing at the great arch, for example, provides commanding views of plazas in both directions, giving students an instant orientation, which he contends will create a sense of well-being.

All such details help the building function as a place that underscores the importance of making students comfortable and encouraging daily, face-to-face contact with colleagues. That's important at a time when education—and indeed, much of professional life—revolves around virtual connections with other humans that take place on a computer screen or via a cell phone. Violich actually sees a strong connection between the social mission of the Steger Center and the desire of students, perhaps unexpressed, for alternatives to the endless, if ethereal, perspectives of the digital world.

"You could argue that technology would be the nemesis of good planning and architecture, because it would mean that students could just huddle behind computers in dorm rooms and never walk outside," Violich says. "But I think that what happens is that because technology tends to limit how one navigates public space, it makes students arguably yearn for face-to-face, voice-to-voice community interaction."

Students aren't the only ones who need to reach beyond the virtual world, which makes the Steger Center significant beyond academia. It could be argued that as the pace of digital communication increases, places that foster real social interaction in such a relaxed, transparent, and lively way will be more important than ever before.

Steven Litt is the art and architecture critic of *The Plain Dealer* in Cleveland, Ohio. He has written for other publications including *Metropolis*, *Planning*, and *ARTnews*. He was a Michigan Journalism Fellow at the University of Michigan, Ann Arbor, and a Helena Rubenstein Fellow at the Whitney Museum of American Art. He lives in Shaker Heights, Ohio, with his wife Rosalie and daughters, Sarah and Elizabeth.

RESTING WITH STYLE AND GRACE — THE JOSEPH A. STEGER STUDENT LIFE CENTER
by Ron Kull

As architects, we generally consider how a building meets the ground—in essence, we design a base that holds the building in place. But we seldom have to design this base while traversing a change in grade of some 50 feet along nearly 500 feet of a building's length.

Yet one building on the campus of the University of Cincinnati creatively demonstrates that a building's base can be much more than just a meeting between building and ground.

The Joseph A. Steger Student Life Center by Moore Ruble Yudell makes a beautiful and varied connection to grade as it extends down Main Street, the winding thoroughfare that is the center of campus. Sometimes the connection to the ground is simple—for example, red brick meeting concrete pavers—and sometimes it is complex, as when a row of columns lifts the façade of the building and creates an arcade for pedestrians.

The Steger Center's south face rambles along Main Street, which bisects the campus from top to bottom. At its back, on the north side, is a classic quadrangle formed by Swift, Baldwin, and Rhodes Halls.

The southern façade, in particular, has a dynamic character that contributes greatly to the quintessentially urban nature of the UC campus. At one end, stadium-style seating carved from Carnelian granite provides numerous places for students to sit and converse with friends, watch passersby, or simply enjoy the warmth of the midday sun. The seats also provide a viewing platform for events and programs taking place on Bearcat Plaza, the center of campus.

Further along, the stairs recede and the base is enhanced by a series of brick columns that raise the zinc-clad mass of the building to accommodate easy access to retail services at street level as well as the upper floors of the building, which house student organizations and student support functions. Just below the grand arch that opens the center of the building and connects it to the quadrangle above, those columns form a cloistered walkway, providing a formal sense of arrival for a campus art gallery and an interesting path for the curious pedestrian.

The Steger Center is part of a trio of buildings that share a common design language and materials (the others being Thom Mayne's Campus Recreation Center and Charles Gwathmey's Tangeman University Center). The Recreation Center and the University Center form the southern edge of Main Street, but since their purposes are different, their bases are less permeable and their assets most evident in their interiors. Therefore, the transparency and variety of the Steger Center make the greatest contribution to the open space that provides Main Street with its urban vibe.

So let's look more deeply into the elements that make the building so successful. While an entrance is often a focal point for a building, the Steger Center has numerous entry points, each with a different character. Additionally, since the building is narrow (only forty feet wide at most points), it has only two important sides, not four. What would typically be the east and west elevations disappear into endpoints reminiscent of a ship's prow. But one might question: how does this work? The west end of the building creates a grand gesture of entry, not into the building but into the space between the Steger Center and Swift Hall to its north. Entrances into the Steger Center and Swift become secondary to this entry between the two buildings, which begins as a carpet of Carnelian granite at McMicken Commons and transitions the grade very gently, incorporating both an accessible ramp and shallow steps. The vertical nature of this entrance is capped by a sawtooth roof that terminates the vertical space and provides a canopy for the bridges that connect the two buildings.

Back on the south face, the shallow steps expand to create the previously described stadium steps, which function as both a "couch" for the campus's living room and as a device for navigating the changing grade. Gradually, these steps move people to the street level, where they can enter the first retail space on Main Street, a business center. Here, the base of the building becomes transparent, and

the concrete pavers that cover Bearcat Plaza extend through the building and create a grand portal, a ceremonial entry and exit to the plaza from the quadrangle behind the Steger Center.

Proceeding east along the south face of the building, a common grade is maintained to permit easy access to the next retail space. In order to accomplish this across the topography, the stadium steps again become the building's footing on the ground, receding only as they reach the building's primary entrance and elevator core. Past this main entrance, the steps again easily provide for the grade differentials that continue along Main Street. Along this route are entrances to street-level offices and the gallery space.

These entrances are enhanced by another unique feature of the building's base—a cloistered walk, or arcade, that produces an intermediate space between the granite stadium steps and the building envelope. The arcade is created by a series of columns that touch the granite steps and lift the building off the ground to the office level one floor above. In order to provide a common floor elevation for the office space, the arcade columns vary in length, gracefully accommodating the tremendous change in grade along Main Street. Not only does the arcade successfully lift the building off the ground, but it permits the building to become fully integrated with the activity on Main Street and creates a quiet interplay of light and shadow for anyone who chooses to enter it.

As the last retail space is approached at the east end of the building, the arcade ends and the steps fall away once again, exposing a simple brick base. Just beyond, the north and south façades come together to create the eastern prow of the building, but not an eastern façade.

This point is also the eastern entrance to the intimate space on the building's north side, which is dramatically different from the open space on Main Street. A narrow void between the center and Baldwin Quadrangle has been transformed into a soft and inviting space known as the Mews Gardens. On this side, a series of terraces address the change in grade and create small gardens filled with

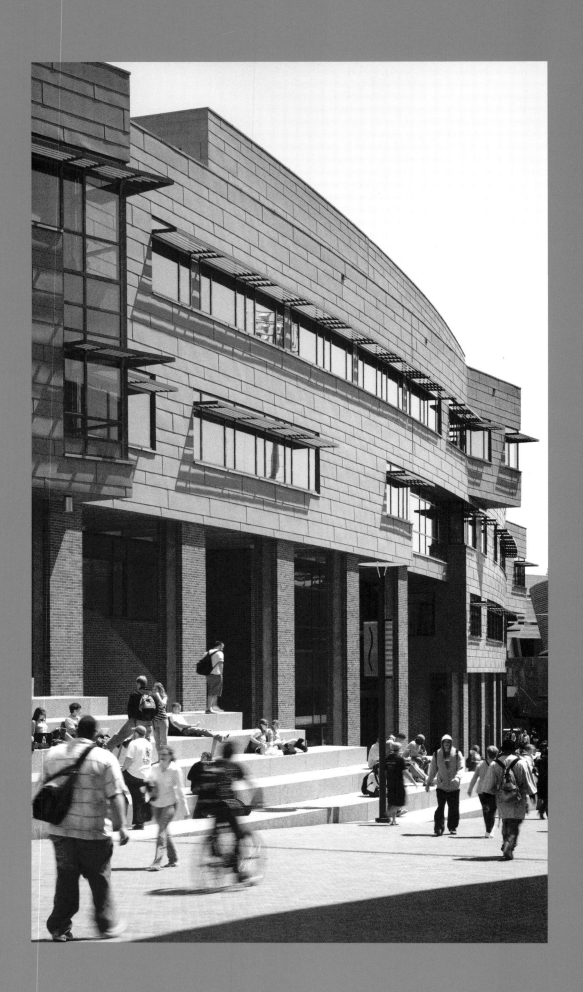

outdoor sculpture and seating spaces for quiet conversation and studying. At the other end of the void, a grand stair rises up and connects visually to the transparent bridges that connect the Steger Center directly with the classrooms in the classical Swift Hall. The northern façade is simple and calm, and the scale reduced. Here, the building's base plays its more traditional role of meeting the ground. There are no arcades or stadium steps, and so the grade variations are dealt with in a different way.

In the Mews Gardens, stairs separate the small gardens and accommodate the grade variations. Throughout the Mews, large glass windows fill much of the space between columns on the building, and light flows out from the interior spaces to enliven the gardens at night. This open relationship, in turn, draws the landscape into the ground floor of the building. Plant material, textured pavement, and architectural artifacts become, in essence, part of the building's base, making it three-dimensional.

And while this function is invisible to most, the Mews also serves a practical purpose: to allow vertical separations between Swift, Baldwin, and Rhodes Halls that are necessary to accommodate truck service lanes, a loading dock, and numerous level variations in adjacent buildings.

One additional element—lighting—adds to the overall impact of this building. On Main Street, subtle lighting is provided by rows of reflective fixtures and borrowed light from interior spaces along both sides of the street. In the Mews, the lighting is primarily provided by the interior of the Steger Center and is only amplified by fixtures hidden in the landscape, maintaining the intimate quality of the space.

The dynamic and varied qualities of the Steger Center play a special role on the University of Cincinnati campus. The southern façade, so strong and active, contributes to the urban edge and energy of Main Street. The northern façade, more reserved and quiet, provides a place for privacy and repose. The combined effect of these elements contributes greatly to the profound sense of place that now defines the University of Cincinnati campus. That the Steger Center does this in ways that don't shout their importance on a first encounter, but rather, reveal themselves over time, only makes the building more remarkable.

Ron Kull, FAIA, has made a notable physical contribution to the development of a public university environment conceived to improve the quality of life on and off campus. Over fifteen years, he led the transformation of the University of Cincinnati's campus to provide a more supportive environment for students, faculty, and staff. As a result, the area is now distinguished by a sense of place that creates lasting positive impressions about campus life and the educational experience at the University of Cincinnati.

PROJECT DESCRIPTION

THE JOSEPH A. STEGER STUDENT LIFE CENTER
University of Cincinnati, Ohio

The Joseph A. Steger Student Life Center and the renovated Swift Hall are part of a new spine of campus activity organized along major pedestrian and topographic paths. The project is part of a multi-building Main Street planned collaboratively within a campus master plan by Hargreaves Associates. It is anchored at one end by Gwathmey Siegel's Tangeman University Center and at the other by a new Campus Recreation Center designed by Morphosis; the Steger Center links the two along a thin, curving site, traversing nearly 600 feet in length and 55 feet of vertical drop. The dense mix of academic, social, and retail uses within the Steger Center provides the community with a district of activity and urbanity not found within most campuses.

ARC OF INTERACTION
The Steger Center evolved as a vessel for movement and interaction. It traverses the site as a long, slender form that encourages parallel movement along a south-facing arcade. Student amenities and organizations have identities and entries along the arcade. The most active day/night uses, such as cafes and computer labs, are located at street level. Key paths of campus movement are reinforced though perpendicular cuts that are literally shortcuts through the building. A series of "found spaces" to the north are shaped as social places between the new building and existing buildings. To the west, a covered atrium is formed between the Steger Center and the older Swift Hall.

BODY LANGUAGE
This collection of spaces adjacent to buildings provides a diversity of domains in which to gather, perch, and move. The spaces celebrate the pleasures of topographic movement and present a wide range of scales, thus heightening one's kinesthetic awareness. The Steger Center itself is a single-loaded building with social corridors along the south side. These recapitulate the movement of the arcade below and are animated by bays for informal gathering. Social stairs are daylit and become focal points for orientation and movement. The building form and fenestration frame are energized by the activities within. The building's bays, galleries, and arcades speak of the dynamic academic and social energy of the place.

TECTONICS OF EARTH AND SKY
The Steger Center is constructed simply and directly. It meets and merges with the earth through a combination of cast-in-place concrete and brick construction at the arcade. A light zinc-and-glass skin emphasizes horizontal movement and reflects the sky. Louvered sunshades protect the major south-facing gathering spaces. A program of boldly colored signage identifies and animates the social role of the building.

The Steger Center connects to the campus at multiple scales though axial movements, framed views, and positively configured open spaces. A richness of habitation arises, in part, from the diversity of scale of places between, adjacent to, and inside the buildings. These present an array of spaces articulated enough to invite habitation, yet flexible and subtle enough for the participants to improvise and vary their scale and type of activity. From the window bay for one or two, to the quiet Mews Gardens, to the large enclosure of the atrium or sweep of the arcade, the inhabitant is engaged in a dynamic interaction with the building and its greater campus setting.

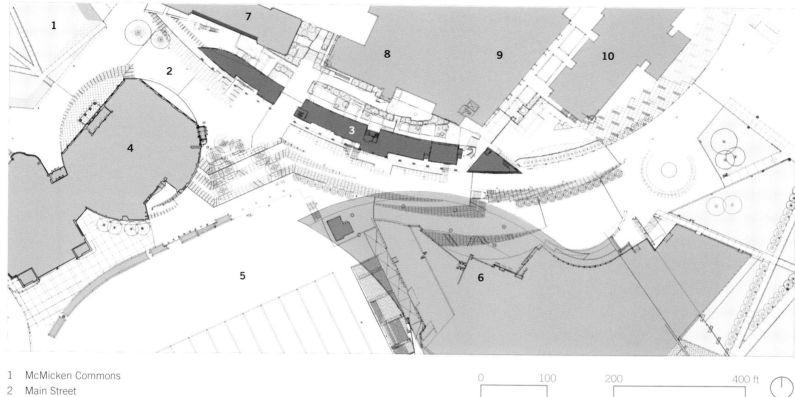

1   McMicken Commons
2   Main Street
3   Steger Student Life Center
4   Tangeman University Center
5   Nippert Stadium
6   Campus Recreation Center
7   Swift Hall
8   Baldwin Hall
9   Rhodes Hall
10 Engineering Research Center

0   100   200   400 ft

PRINCIPLES

WEAVING THE BRAID

Over several years, the campus representatives and Hargreaves Associates developed a planning strategy that involved weaving campus pathways, based on topography and pedestrian movement, to connect and give shape to a formerly disaggregated campus.

This pattern of paths and connections became known as the Campus Braid. It facilitated movement through the campus through its reinforcement of existing topography. The area of greatest potential confluence of uses was identified as the future Main Street for the campus.

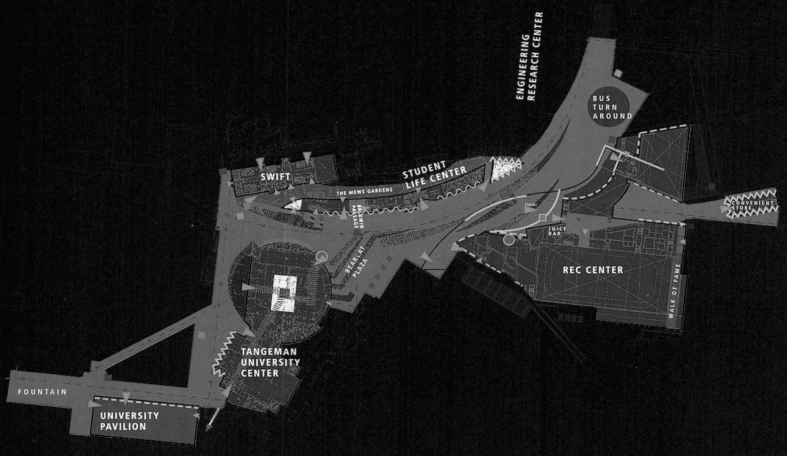

Mapping nighttime uses and lighting

MAIN STREET AS 24/7 CONNECTOR

The Main Street sector of the campus was planned to create an intensity of day/night uses along the Campus Braid. The planning and shaping of each building strengthened its relationship to adjacent buildings, landscape, and campus context. The design team and campus staff chose to create compact, densely planned buildings and open spaces to enhance opportunities for interaction and for the nurturing of community.

Shaping and carving the Joseph A. Steger Student Life Center in relation to key campus paths serves to revitalize these paths as well as to strengthen the visual and cultural connections to other parts of campus, such as Schneider Quad and the Engineering Research Center.

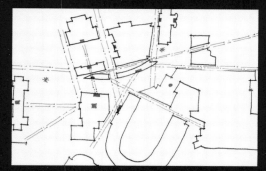

Axes and entries

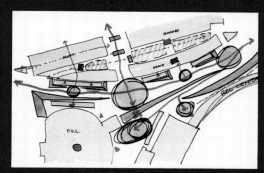

Axes and places

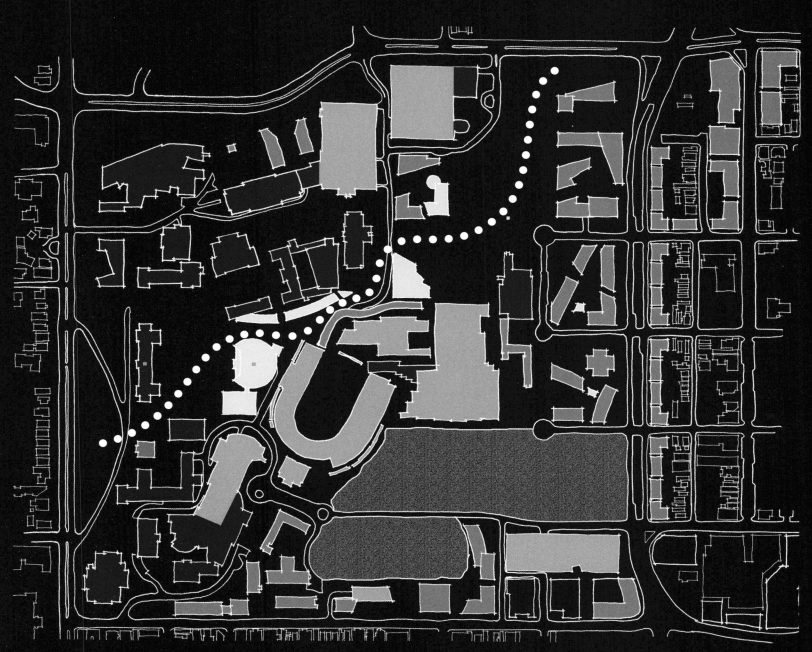

Campus Braid: linking old and new

MAIN STREET AS PLACE-MAKING

At the inception of the project, the campus had already been raising the level of aspiration for its architecture and accomplished this through the commissioning of individual iconic buildings. While buildings by Eisenman, Graves, Gehry, and Pei Cobb Freed had sharply increased the quality and excitement of campus architecture, the university felt that it had not generated buildings where the spaces and places between buildings were creating community and campus. The new Main Street was identified as the opportunity for this collaborative planning initiative.

DYNAMIC COLLABORATION

During the early collaboration, the design team worked with students, faculty, and staff to imagine and test alternate programs and their distribution. For the students, boundaries of time and academic discipline were disappearing. This encouraged the development of a denser, more varied mix of uses within the Main Street district. Academic, residential, recreational, retail, entertainment, and student program uses were aggregated more compactly that in any other part of campus.

By working collaboratively on site planning and programming for the Main Street district, the design team was able to achieve critical synergies that established a range of campus paths and places.

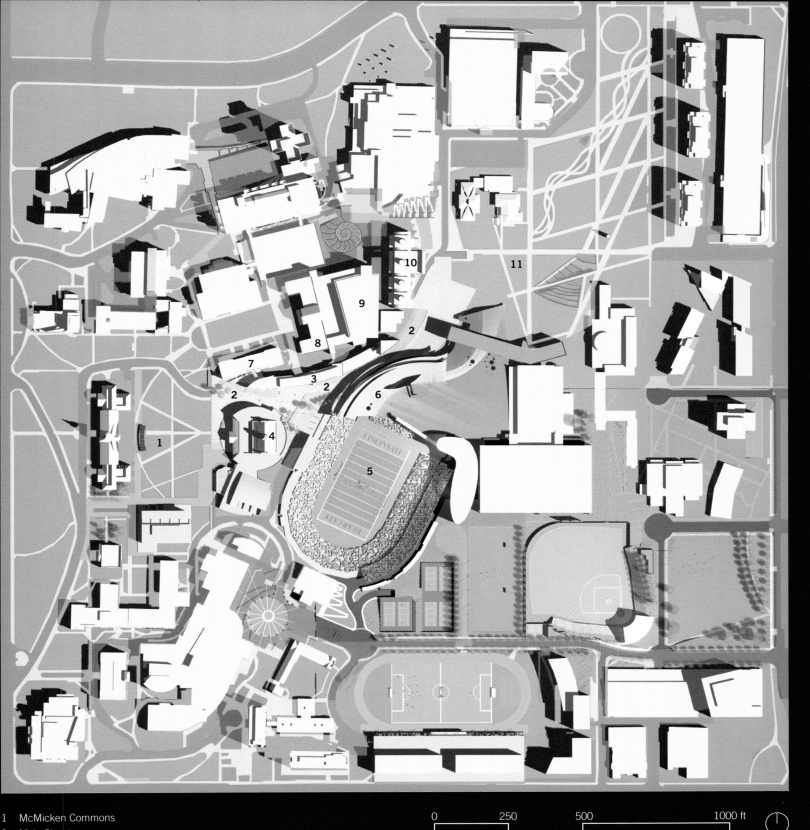

1 McMicken Commons
2 Main Street
3 Steger Student Life Center
4 Tangeman University Center
5 Nippert Stadium
6 Campus Recreation Center
7 Swift Hall
8 Baldwin Hall
9 Rhodes Hall
10 Engineering Research Center
11 Campus Green

BUILDING AS PLACE-MAKING
Within the richness of the Main Street project, the Steger Center was conceived and planned as a rich piece of campus and urban fabric. It was shaped to interact with the campus context as well as with each of its neighbors in order to create paths and places that weave a richer campus context, nurture interaction, and support community.

BUILDING ORGANIZATION
The building is organized as a kind of flexible loft. Building systems are gathered together with vertical circulation to create permanent entryways. The structure uses cast-in-place concrete columns and slabs to create a sturdy and economical shell. Mechanical distribution and lighting are exposed, and furnishing is modular and flexible. As a whole, the building is conceived as a flexible armature, which should accommodate change over time.

HIERARCHY OF PLACES IN THE BUILDING
In addition to the development of flexibility within the building, it was important to create a diversity of scales and place typologies. Common spaces include paths (the exterior arcade, interior street, and stair entryways) and places (common lounges, terraces, balconies, and bays). Path and place intersect at the most public parts of the building, such as two-story lounges or the vertical intersection between the graduate-student lounge and the two-story Starbucks cafe. These spaces occur at multiple scales to accommodate a range of activities and needs. They serve the "unprogrammed" needs of the community, which are often underserved due to the way buildings are typically programmed, funded, and designed.

The more conventionally programmed spaces are contained within the clear-span lofts of the building. They accommodate a range of uses, from student organizations to academic, cultural, and retail spaces. These areas are particularly flexible in plan. They are more differentiated in section, allowing for a public-to-private gradient from the Main Street level upwards.

SINGLE-LOADED FOR LIGHT AND MOVEMENT
The building is organized so that movement occurs on the south or Main Street side. The social interaction of Main Street is thus recapitulated on the upper level, where "interior streets" encourage interaction and views to and from the building. This social street is animated by daylight and by the articulation of common spaces, entries, and bays for informal meeting and lounging.

The thin section of the building assures that daylighting is optimized throughout.

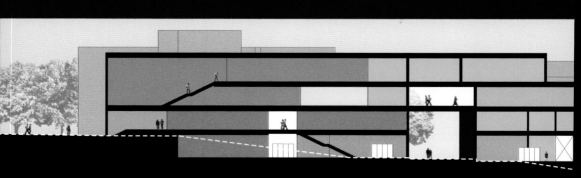

A RICH COLLECTION OF PUBLIC PLACES

The public places shaped by the buildings of Main Street are diverse in scale and type. They include:

- Places along the edges of buildings: arcades, covered porches, entry areas and thresholds, balconies, bays
- Places between buildings: streets, plazas, Mews Gardens, atria
- Places carved out of buildings: portals, passages
- Places on top of buildings: roof terraces

Diagram: Kit of Parts

1   Mechanical Penthouse
2   Office Suite
3   Loft Office
4   Common Space
5   Social Stair
6   Mechanical Core
7   Brick Base
8   Exterior Arcade and "Interior Street"
9   Zinc Clad Curtain Wall
10 Sun Shade
11 "Eyebrow" Bay

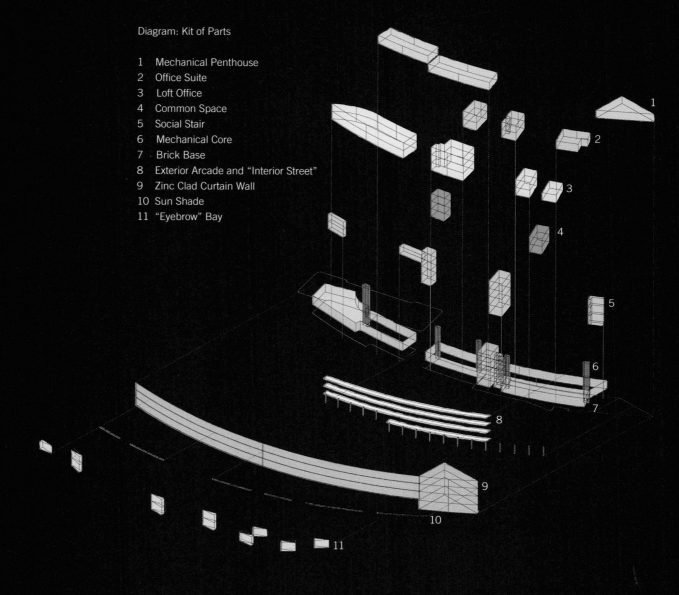

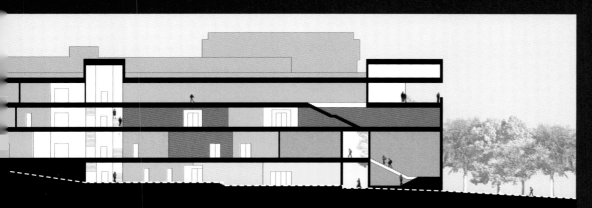

Art Museum
Professional Practice
Computer Lab
Conference Center
Global Studies
Student Government
Student Organizations
Food
Retail
Ethnic Studies
Wellness
OMBUDS

LINKING AND COVERING
The physical linkage to and remodeling of the old Swift Hall building created the opportunity for an unanticipated synergy. The combination of bridging to Swift at two levels, and connecting and covering with a new canopy, created a powerful new arrival and atrium space that marks the beginning of Main Street on the south and the new Mews Gardens on the north. By carefully inserting the zinc skin onto the renovated part of the south Swift elevation, new and old are woven together, but each retains its identity. The brick base of the Steger Center both connects to the ground and converses with Swift. The lightweight zinc skin above connects to Gwathmey Siegel's Tangeman University Center and the Morphosis Campus Recreation Center. It also links to the sky and to the changing light above.

WEAVING PATH AND PLACE
The terraced Mews Gardens to the north of the Steger Center solved complex adjacency issues while creating unanticipated new program opportunities. To the north lie the service areas of Rhodes Hall. The original Hargreaves Master Plan anticipated laminating the Steger Center against the existing lab building. When we pulled the new building south, moving closer to the Campus Recreation Center, we discovered that we could create a more dynamic relationship with the Morphosis project, while setting up the opportunity for quiet "back" or secondary spaces to the north.

Solar studies allayed concerns about the light levels of the northern spaces. Working carefully with the topography and the terracing of retaining walls, we were able to create a series of discrete, quiet courtyards woven together by stairs and accessible ramps. The adjacent loading dock was screened and tempered by landscape and walls.

This set of paths and places has become one of the most valued on campus, providing a more secluded counterpoint to the life of Main Street.

CHOREOGRAPHY: MOVEMENT IN SPACE AND TIME
The movement of individuals and groups through space and time is one key component of supporting serendipitous social interaction. The shaping of paths and places both inside and between buildings can stimulate a richer experience of place and a more vital social context. Creating multiple kinds of paths and optimizing the intersections of paths and places in both the horizontal and vertical dimensions can also encourage a kind of three-dimensional social plaid of opportunity and interaction. Further, designing places in close dialogue with natural topography can enhance our kinesthetic connection to the place and environment, as well as strengthen the connection between building and landscape.

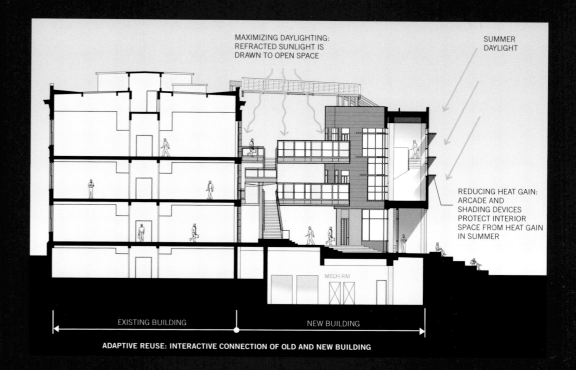

MAXIMIZING DAYLIGHTING:
REFRACTED SUNLIGHT IS
DRAWN TO OPEN SPACE

SUMMER
DAYLIGHT

REDUCING HEAT GAIN:
ARCADE AND
SHADING DEVICES
PROTECT INTERIOR
SPACE FROM HEAT GAIN
IN SUMMER

MECH. RM

EXISTING BUILDING   NEW BUILDING

ADAPTIVE REUSE: INTERACTIVE CONNECTION OF OLD AND NEW BUILDING

BUILDING SUSTAINABILITY AND ADAPTIVE REUSE

The building is shaped to optimize daylighting. A slim building depth allows natural light and views to penetrate over 75% of occupied areas, reducing lighting loads during the day. Building orientation—long façades facing primarily north or south—allow windows to be easily shaded by overhangs or sun shades where required. Low-e glass, frit glass, and deeply set windows further reduce the amount of sun entering the building, which in turn reduces the mechanical cooling required. Passive strategies such as providing operable windows to allow cross-ventilation, exposed structure, and thermal mass are essential to building comfort and energy efficiency.

The Steger Center is shaped for flexibility. The structural bay was determined to accommodate a standard office module along the perimeter, and sufficient depth to accommodate a variety of suite sizes and configurations. Early planning for the integration and distribution of building systems allow for large areas of column-free "loft" space. Exposed structural columns and beams, and floors of polished concrete in public circulation areas provide durable surfaces and high ceilings with an efficient use of building materials.

The siting of the building follows sustainable practices. The effect of the building footprint is offset by extensive use of planted areas and permeable paving in the Mews. Lightly colored roof surfaces reduce the building's heat island effect. Ground-floor arcades, through-building passages, and carefully positioned stairways are designed to encourage pedestrian movement along, up, and through the building. Extensive areas of glazing along the ground-floor spaces and the illuminated atrium canopy glow at night, contributing light to the Mews and Main Street while reducing the need for additional outdoor lamps.

Optimized energy performance and controls; the use of sustainable, recycled, low-VOC, and regional materials; the reuse of architectural building fragments saved from demolished campus structures; as well as plans to manage construction waste and storm water all helped the building to achieve its LEED® (Leadership in Energy and Environmental Design) certification.

INHABITING: PERMANENCE AND CHANGE

The building and its adjacent spaces are designed to create a legible spine of movement, program, and places within the core of the campus. The strength and permanence of this armature are balanced by the inherent invitation to use places flexibly. This flexibility of habitation supports change, improvisation, and discovery over time and space.

DRAWINGS

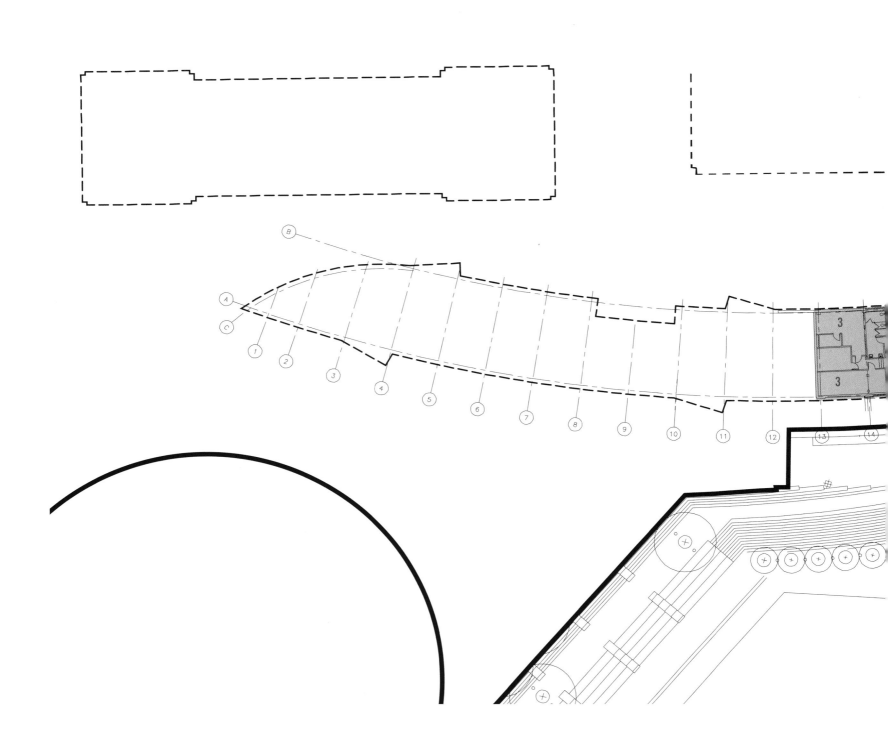

0   25   50   100 ft

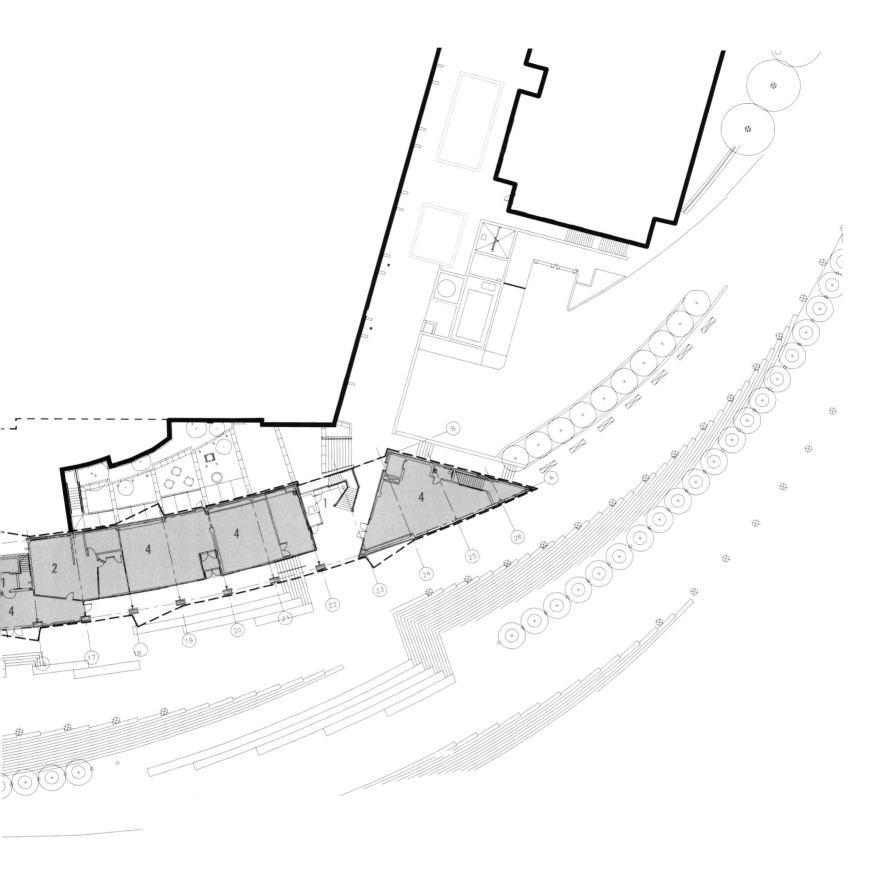

400-LEVEL PLAN

1   Circulation
2   Offices
3   Mech/Service Areas
4   Public (Meeting Rooms, Lounges, Galleries, Dining)

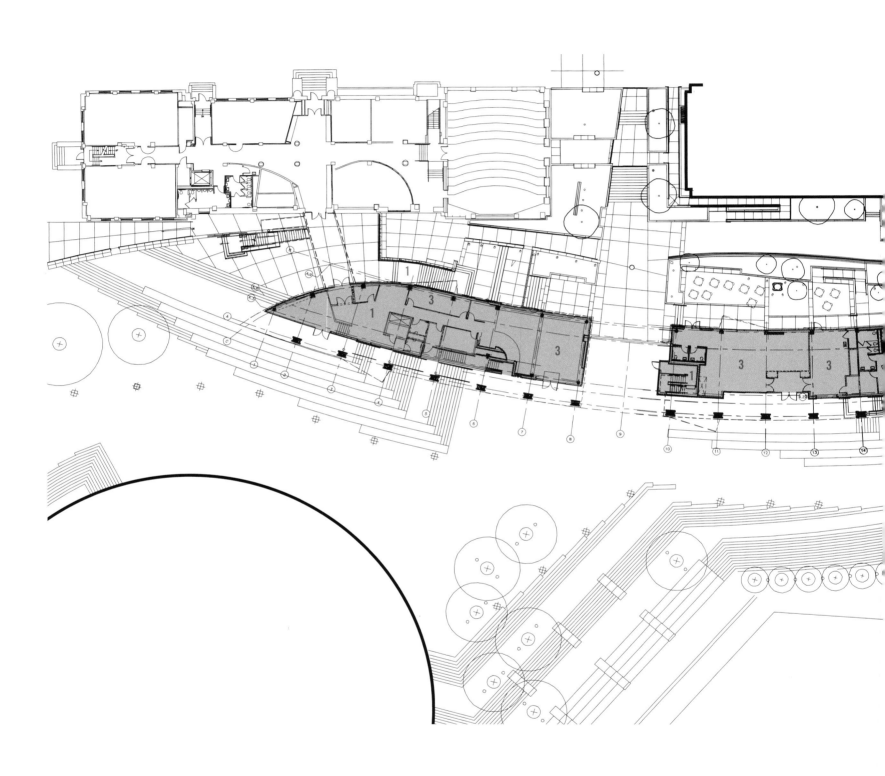

0   25   50   100 ft

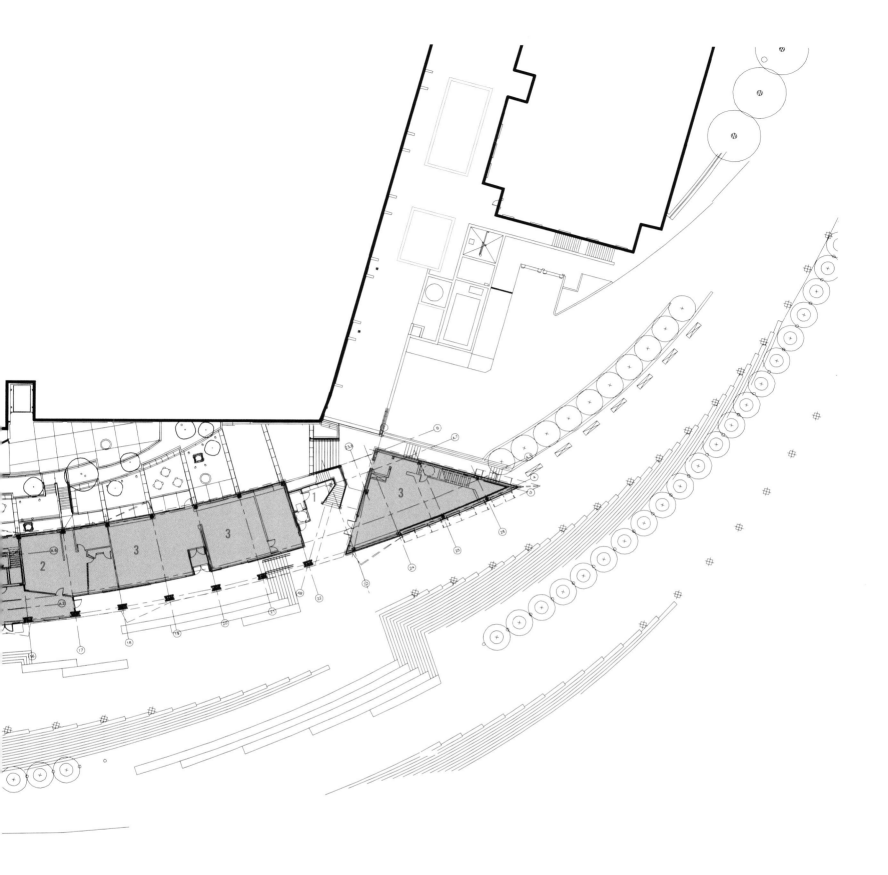

COMPOSITE GRADE-LEVEL PLAN

1   Circulation
2   Offices
3   Public (Meeting Rooms, Lounges, Galleries, Dining)

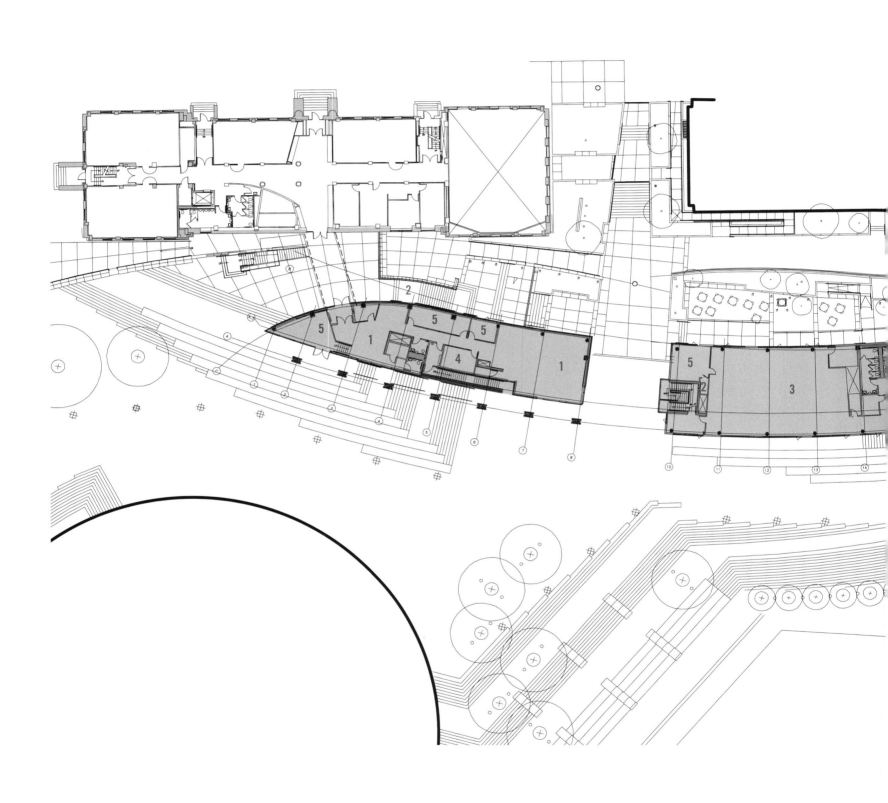

0   25   50   100 ft

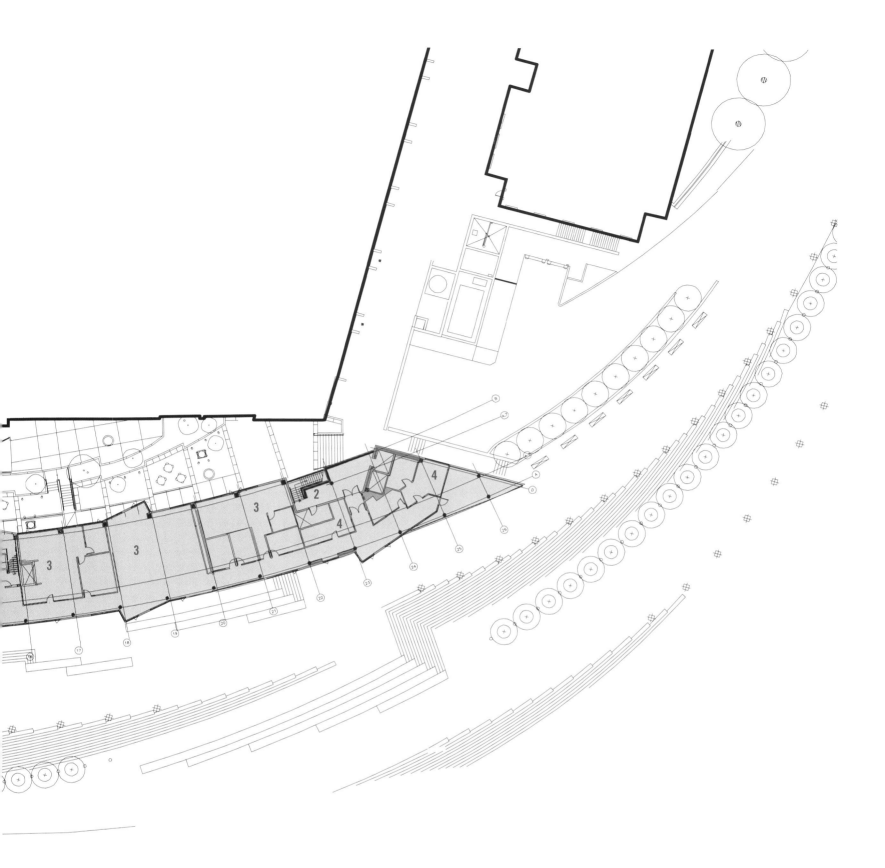

600-LEVEL PLAN

1 Computer Labs
2 Circulation
3 Offices
4 Mech/Service Areas
5 Public (Meeting Rooms, Lounges, Galleries, Dining)

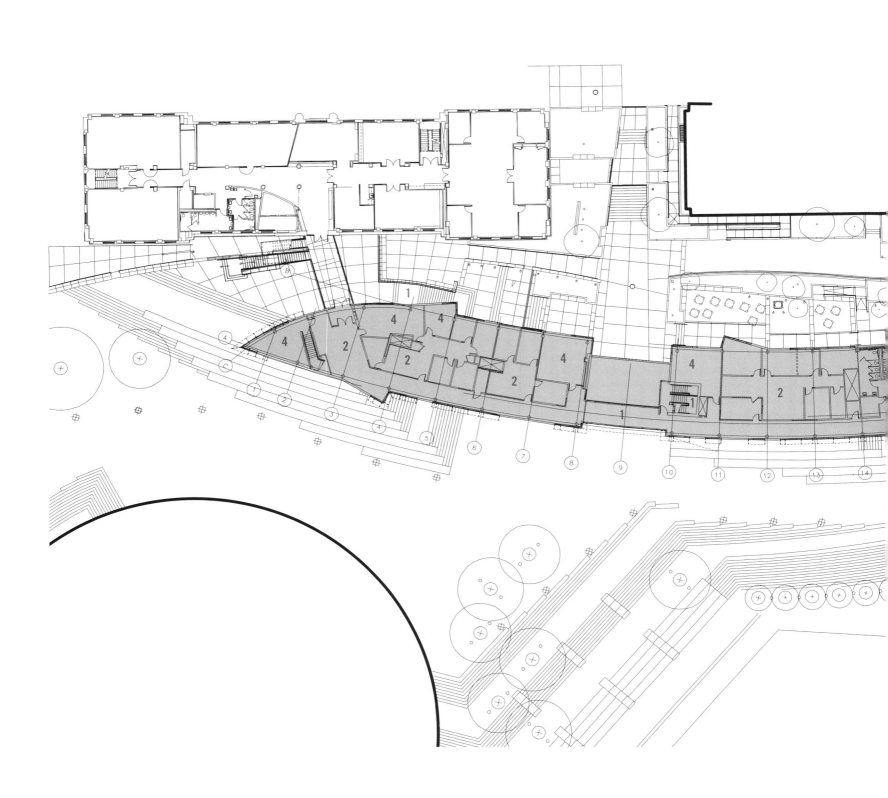

0   25   50   100 ft

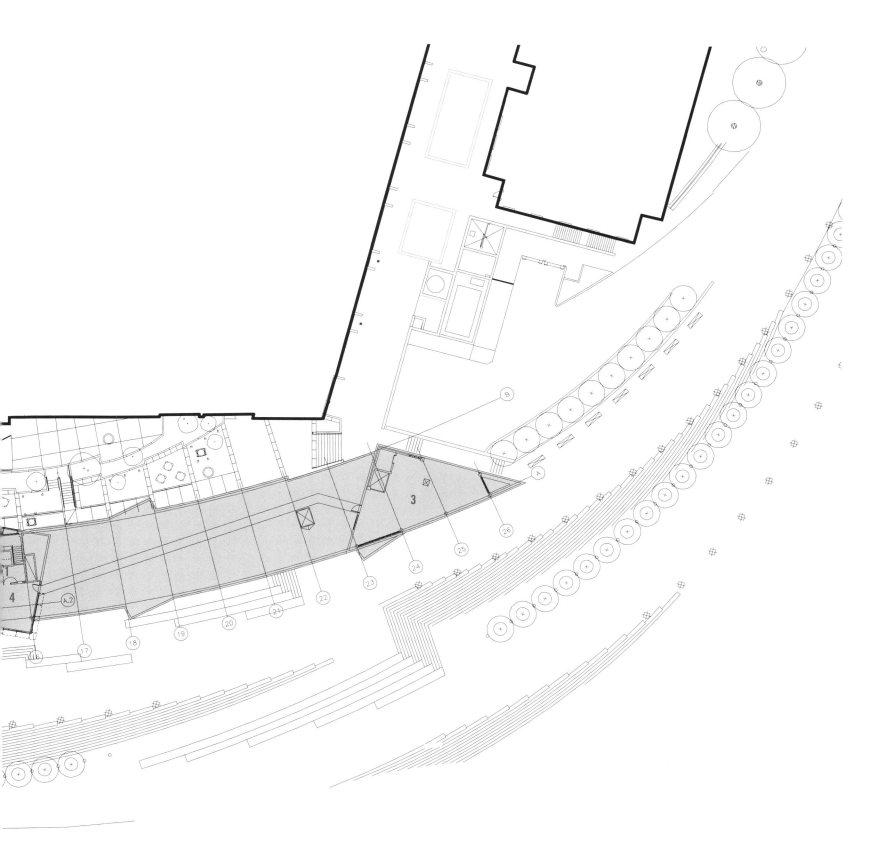

700-LEVEL PLAN

1   Circulation
2   Offices
3   Mech/Service Areas
4   Public (Meeting Rooms, Lounges, Galleries, Dining)

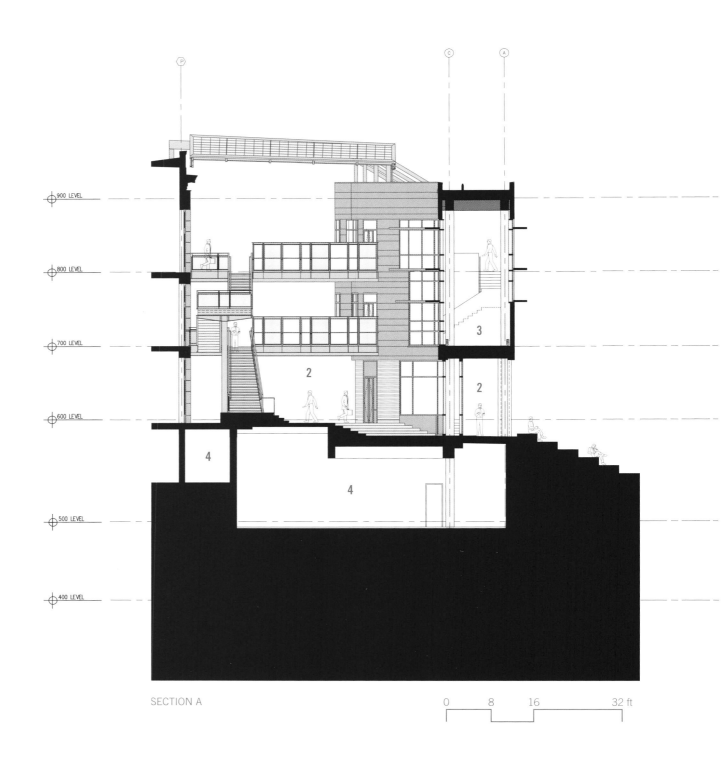

900 LEVEL

800 LEVEL

3

700 LEVEL

2

2

600 LEVEL

4

4

500 LEVEL

400 LEVEL

SECTION A

0   8   16   32 ft

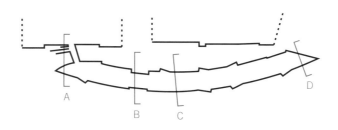

A   B   C   D

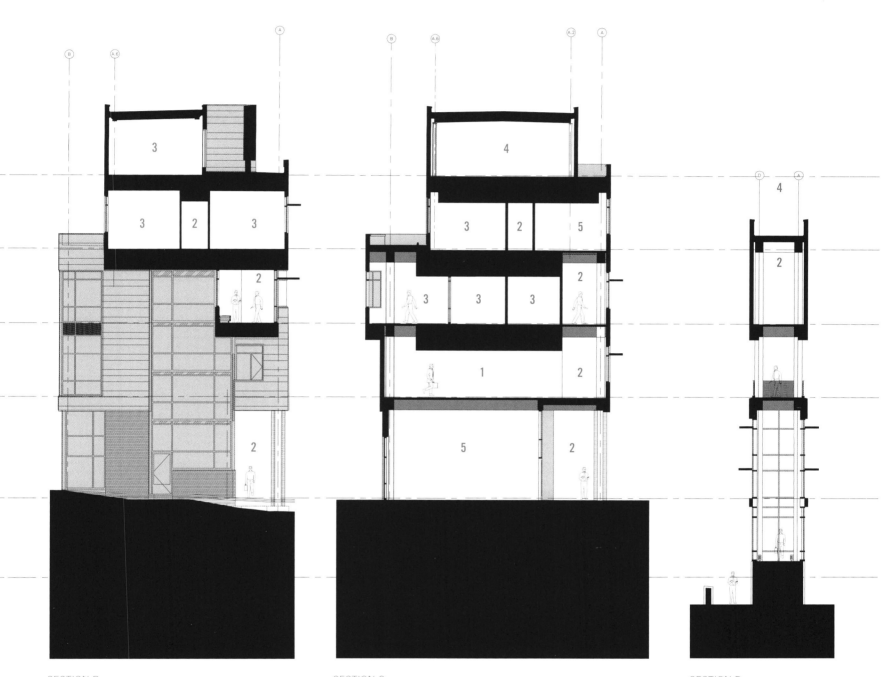

SECTION B   SECTION C   SECTION D

SECTIONS

1   Computer Labs
2   Circulation
3   Offices
4   Mech/Service Areas
5   Public (Meeting Rooms, Lounges, Galleries, Dining)

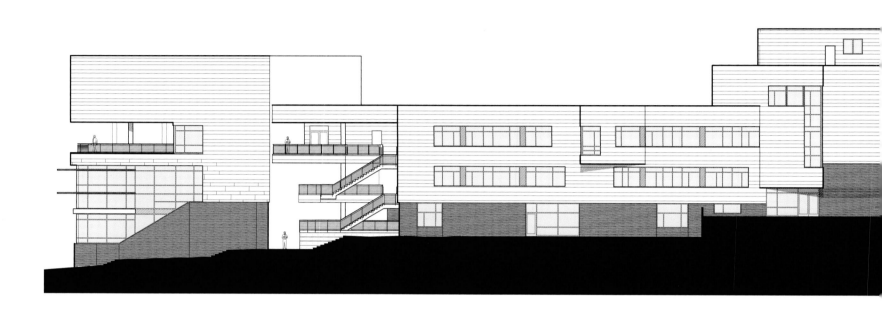

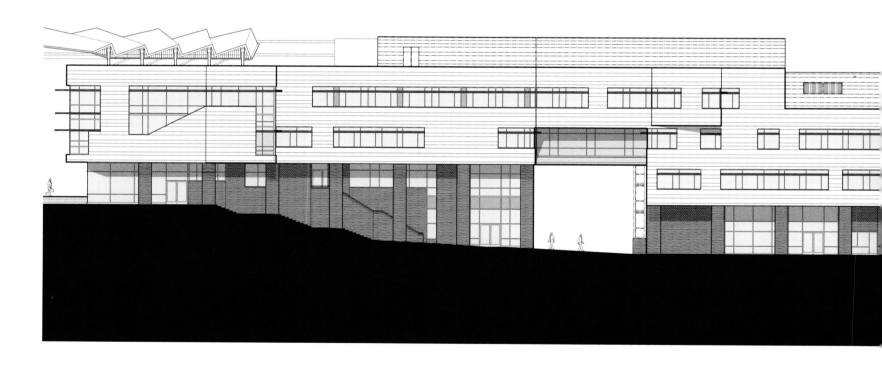

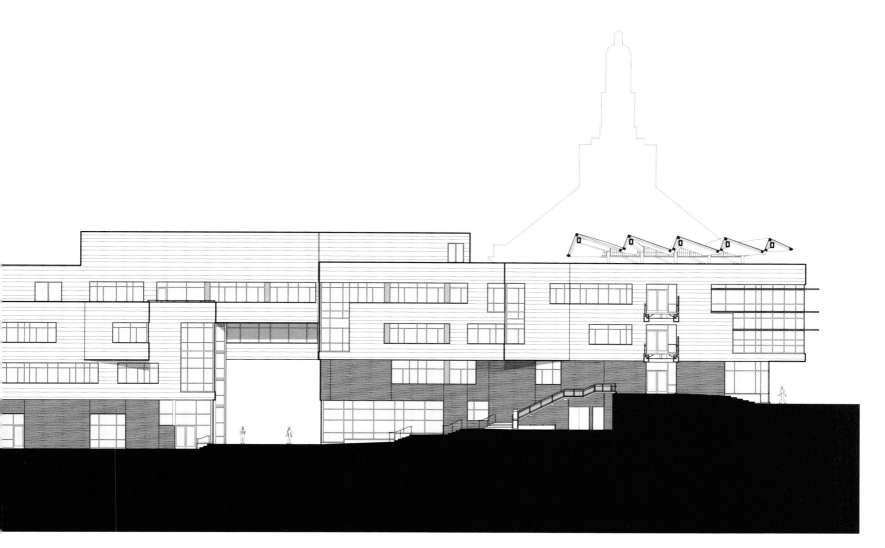

NORTH ELEVATION

SOUTH ELEVATION

0   20   40   80 ft

PHOTOGRAPHS

EAST PROW

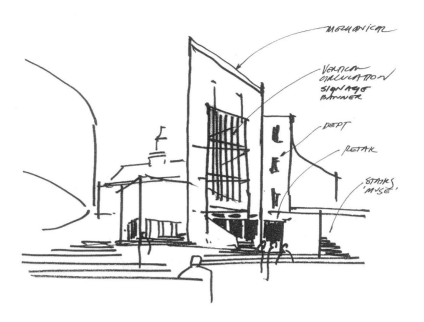

This and previous spread: The prow of the Steger Center (right) and Recreation Center (left) mark the east end of the Main Street axis. A secondary and parallel axis emerges between the Steger Center and adjacent existing buildings through a series of low, brick-clad walls and landscaped terraces into the Mews Gardens.

Above: An early sketch envisioned cross-axial passageways for lateral movement through the building at multiple levels.

Right: During the evening, ambient light from the east prow of the Steger Center and adjacent buildings animates Main Street.

To find out about all the MainStreet events add "UC MainStreet" to you

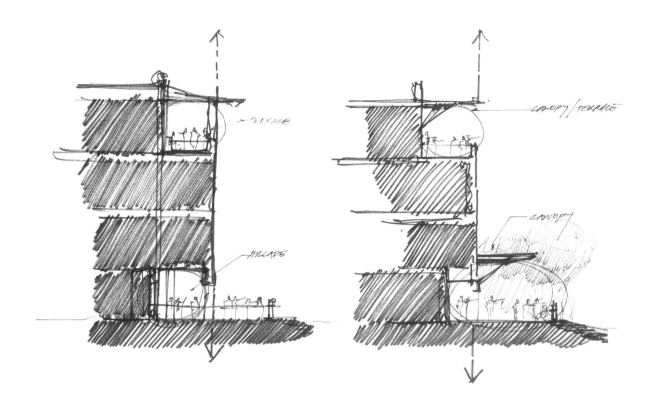

TERRACE

ARCADE

CANOPY / TERRACE

CANOPY

Left: The transparency of the east prow provides a
visually seamless line between a campus coffee shop
and adjacent public spaces.

Above: The southern face of the Steger Center is
carved at its base and top, allowing for visible and
active uses to be seen.

EAST PROW

Previous spread: The descending topography sweeps between the narrow passage between the Steger Center and Recreation Center, framing the distant views of Bearcat Plaza and the Tangeman University Center.

Left and above: Student services, including a two-story lounge and coffee shop, overlook Main Street and adjacent campus public spaces.

MAIN STREET

JOSEPH A. STEGER STUDENT LIFE CENTER

JOHN and DOROT
HERMANIES PRESS

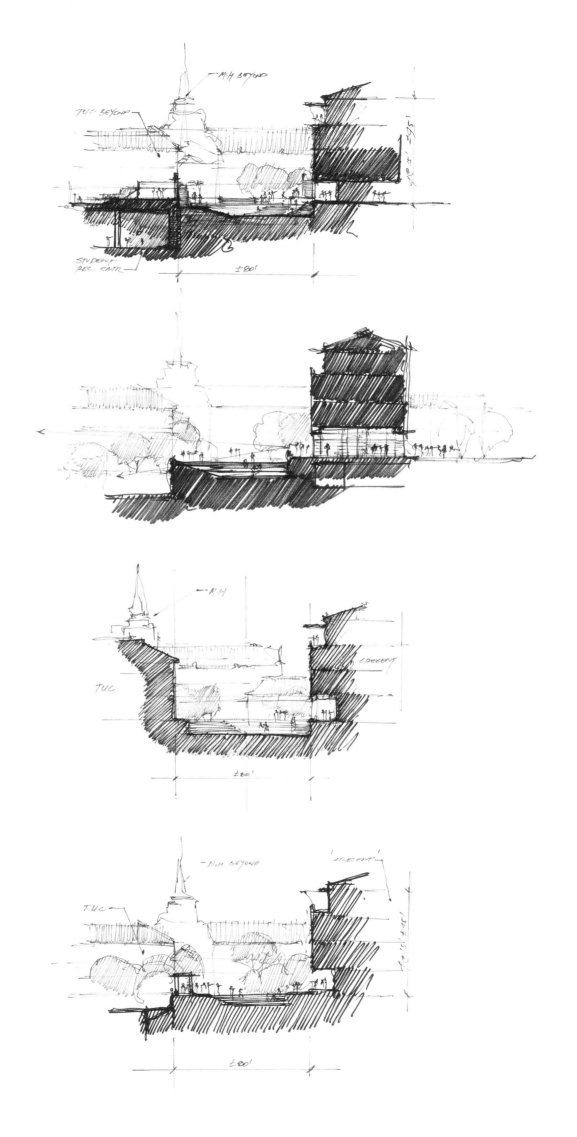

Left: As seen from the adjacent Recreation Center, a
ribbon of student services is tucked behind an arcade
and passageways activating Main Street at street level.

Above: An exploration of the sectional profile of the
Main Street axis, continuously varied with open, closed,
and permeable edge conditions.

MAIN STREET

A single-loaded corridor expands movement along the upper levels of the Steger Center. Habitable bay windows allow for places to perch and observe Main Street in its greater campus context.

Main Street expands into a shared plaza at its midpoint. Low walls negotiate the sloping topography, creating an informal amphitheater. A passageway and bridge frame the campus's historic academic ridge beyond.

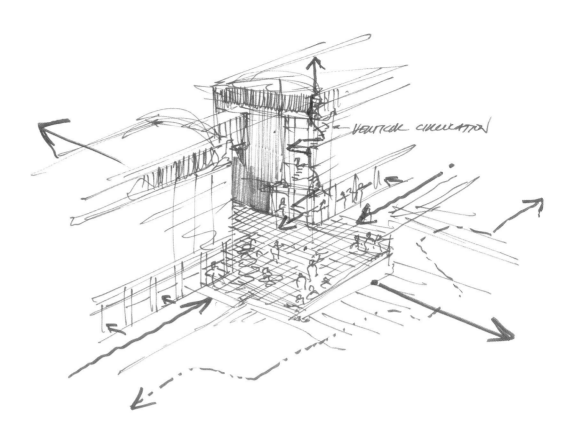

VERTICAL CIRCULATION

Left: Main Street: A south-facing arcade and informal, built-in bench seating provide a variety of spaces for informal gathering. Student amenities and organizations have identities and entries along the arcade.

Above: The sectional profile of the Steger Center varies as it meets street grade. A permeable edge allows for pedestrian movement within, through, and alongside its footprint.

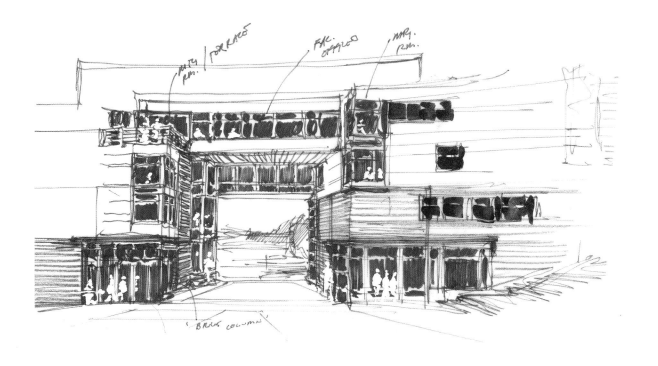

Right: The Baldwin Passage links the historic academic quad, across the Mews Gardens, to Main Street and Bearcat Plaza.

Left: The articulated floor of Main Street weaves between the arcade and passageways, creating a range of places to see and be seen.

Above: The south-facing social corridor is punctuated by bay windows with views to Main Street and the greater campus. Built-in window seats create the opportunity for informal social interaction and study.

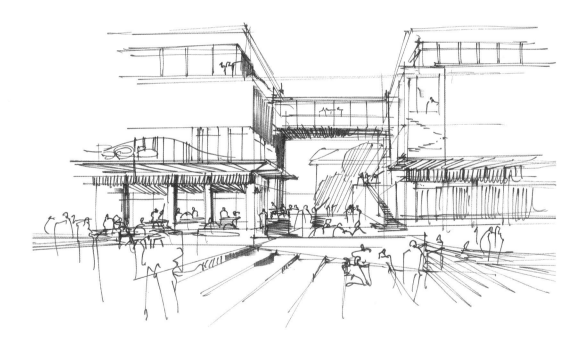

Above and right: Baldwin Passage frames a view to Main Street, Tangeman University Center, and the Music Center beyond.

Left: The multi-level arcade negotiates the
steep topography of Main Street while linking
student programs.

Above: The west prow of the Steger Center reaches
the academic ridge.

Right: An interior, upper-level entry to the Student
Organizations Department overlooks Main Street.
Interior and exterior spaces alternate along the
building's more public and active southern façade.

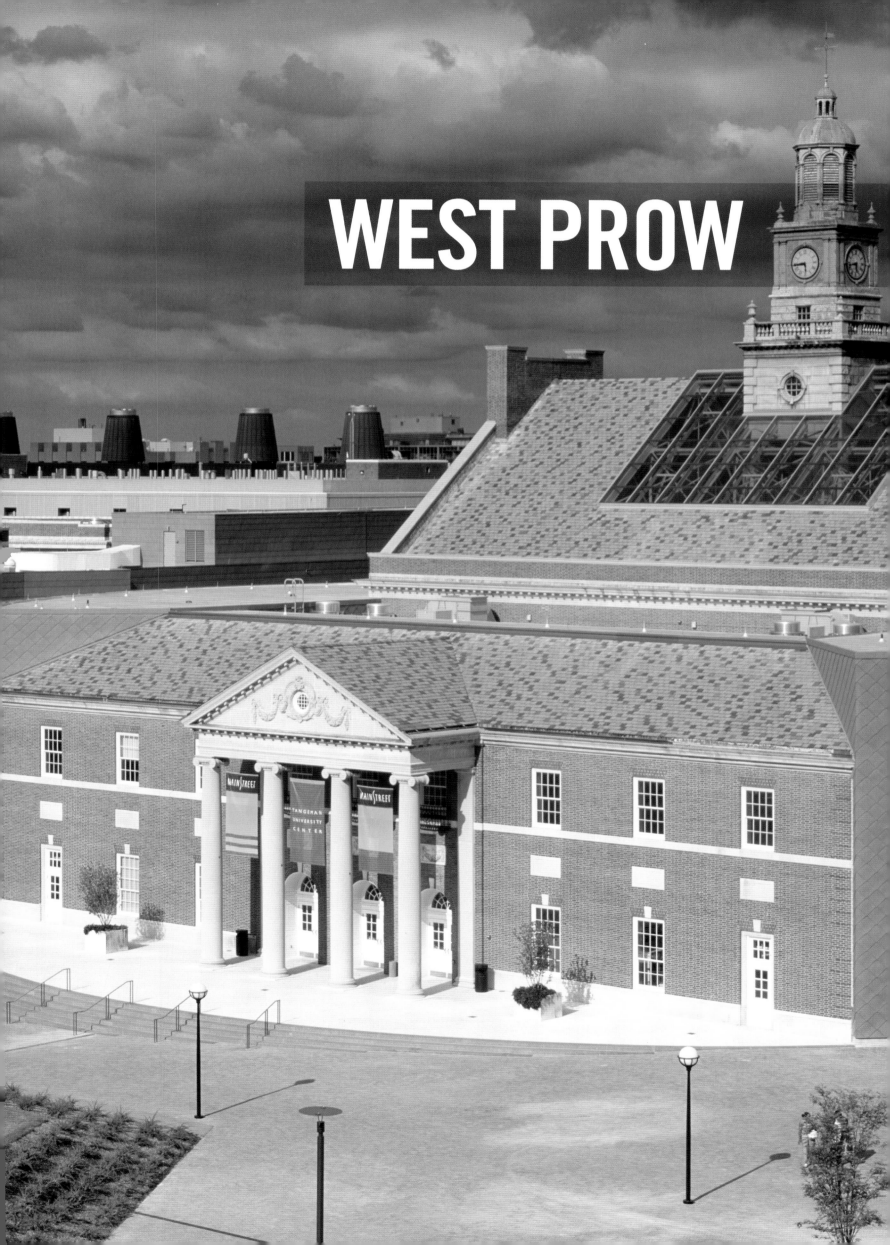

WEST PROW

Previous spreads: The Steger Center's west prow uses a broad canopy, bridges, stairway, and its zinc skin to link to the existing Swift Hall.

Left and above: The Steger Center and the Tangeman University Center frame a narrow passage to Main Street. The west prow of the Steger Center reveals a range of movement spaces and programmatic elements.

Previous spread: The west end of the Steger Center bridges to an existing classroom building, creating a gateway and front-door presence facing the West Commons.

Following spread: The 24-hour computer-center lounge fronts the West Commons and the historic McMicken Hall beyond.

Left and above: Daylight permeates the narrow, interior west prow, suspended above Main Street. Interior finishes utilize industrial materials including cast-in-place concrete columns, concrete floors, and exposed mechanical systems.

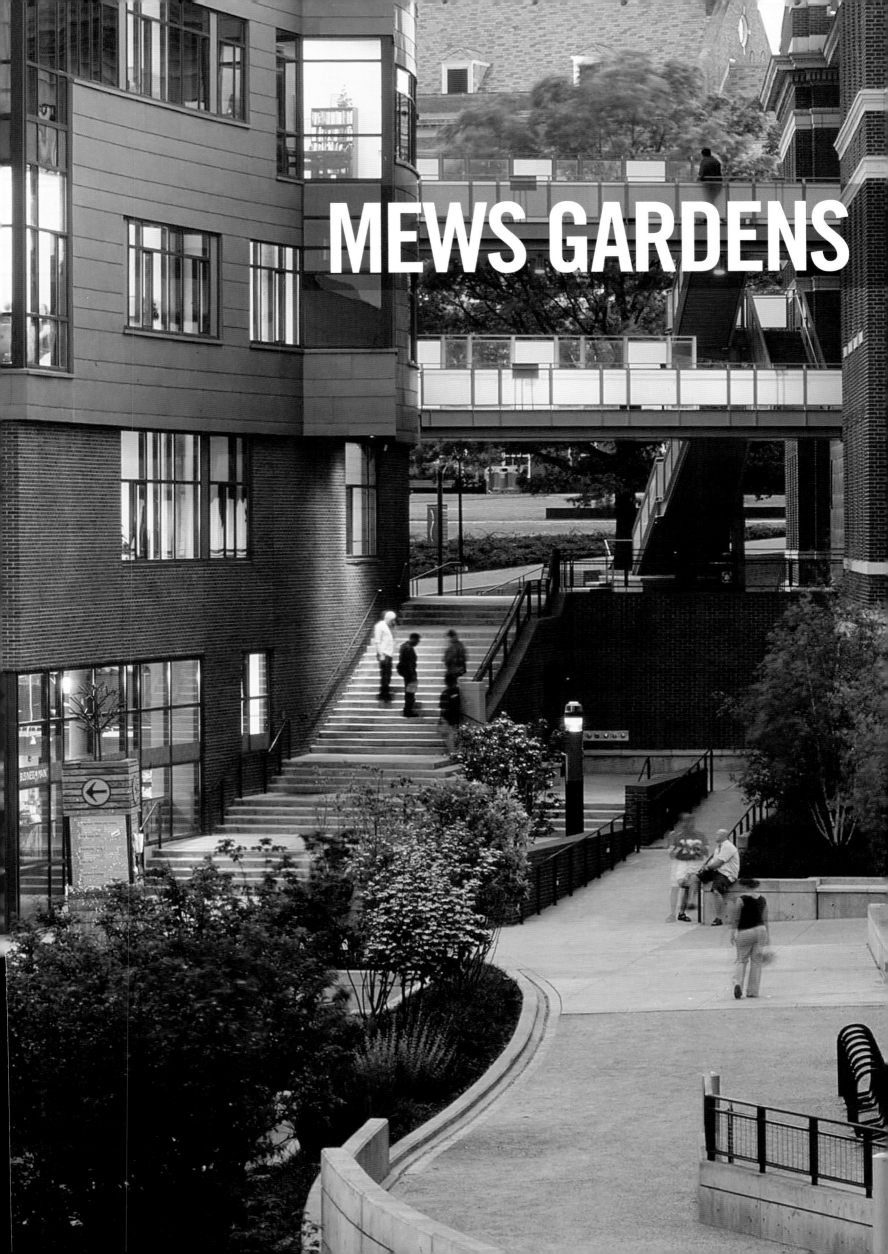

MEWS GARDENS

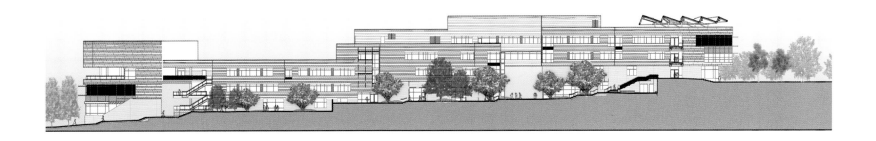

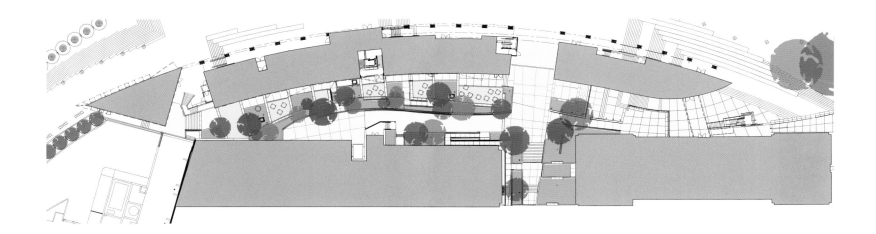

Right and previous spread: The space between the new Steger Center (left) and existing Swift hall (right) frames unfolding views to the campus beyond.

Above: The Mews Gardens and service access are carved out of a narrow 600' long x 40' wide residual space between the Steger Center and adjacent classrooms and buildings. The sectional elevation shows the 60' grade differential.

Left: The terraced Mews Gardens together with bridges,
canopies, and bay windows weave together existing
Swift Hall and the Steger Center, combining to create a
range of movement spaces to socialize, study, and relax.

MEWS GARDENS

This and following spread: The Mews Gardens allow for a
diversity of domains in which to perch, gather, and move.
They celebrate the pleasures of topographic movement and
present a wide range of scales, heightening one's kinesthetic
awareness both in the gardens and within the building.

This spread: Program spaces such as the University Art Museum and adjacent stairways are oriented toward the Mews Gardens, allowing users to see and be seen.

Following spread: Moving through transitional spaces, canopies and bridges weave the Mews Gardens and adjacent existing buildings while framing views to the academic commons beyond. Garden terraces combine to create a three-dimensional "green ribbon" linking the outdoor rooms.

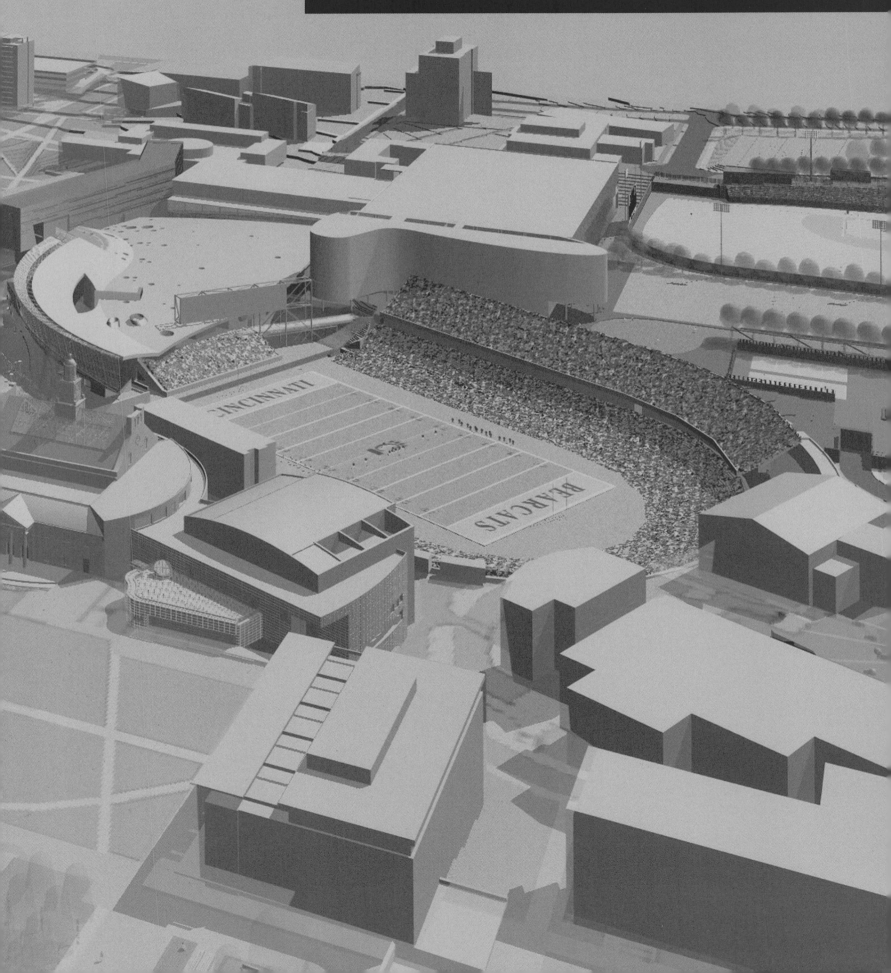

APPENDIX

CREDITS

Joseph A. Steger Student Life Center
University of Cincinnati

Client: Campus Planning, University of Cincinnati
University Architect: Ron Kull, AIA, AUA
Assistant Vice President and Director, Housing: Frank Bowen
Assistant Vice President and Director: Ray Renner
Associate Vice President, Enrollment Management: Stan Henderson
Associate Vice Presidents, Student Affairs and Human Resources: Mauricio Gonzalez,
Tom Hadley, Mitch Livingston
Campus Landscape Architect: Len Thomas
Director, Department of Athletics: Kim Schmidt
Director, General Business Services: Steve Sayers
Director, Campus Planning: Niraj Dangoria
Planner: Ellen Guerrettaz, AIA
Project Managers: Greg Robinson, Pete Luken, Bob Marton
Senior Architect: Chuck Darling
Senior Vice President and Provost: Tony Perzigian
Vice President, Finance: Dale McGirr

Design Architect: Moore Ruble Yudell Architects & Planners
Partner-in-Charge: Buzz Yudell, FAIA
Collaborating Partner: John Ruble, FAIA
Principal-in-Charge: Mario Violich, AIA, ASLA
Project Manager/Associate-in-Charge: Adam Padua, Assoc. AIA, LEED® AP
Color/Materials: Tina Beebe, Kaoru Orime, Yana Khudyakova
Models: Mark Grand, Don Hornbeck
Project Team: Bob Dolbinski, AIA, Alberto Reano, Ted Kane, Alexis Bennett, Ross Morishige
Digital Illustrations: Ross Morishige and glaserworks

Mews Gardens Design: Moore Ruble Yudell with glaserworks

Associate Architect: glaserworks
Partner-in-Charge: Art Hupp III, AIA
Principal: Mike Moose
Project Managers: Steve Haber, Michael Maltinsky
Project Team: Evan Eagle, Rick Fohl, Paul Duffy, Mark Schaffhauser, Len Harding,
David Schmidt, Vicki Whitley, Renea Whittle, Anthony Salvador, Philip Buchy

General Contractor: Dugan & Meyers Construction Company
President: Jay Meyers

Main Street Master Plan and Landscape Architect: Hargreaves Associates
Partner-in-Charge: George Hargreaves, FASLA
Principal-in-Charge: Mary Margaret Jones, Glen Allen
Project Manager: Ken Haines, Principal
Project Team: Katherine Miller, Christopher Reed

Structural: Arup
Associate Principal/Project Manager: Catherine Wells, SE
Project Team: David Milner, Surinder Mann, Kyojin Kim, Henry Medina, Chung-Chi Chu, Chuan Do
Structural Consultant: THP Limited
Project Team: Shayne Manning, Brad Saalfeld, Mike Lewis, Bill Shandersky

Mechanical/Electrical: Arup
Associate Principal: Catherine Wells, SE
Project Manager: Matt Volgyi
Project Team: Zoltan Mezei, James Kirby, Vahik Davoudi

MEP Consultant: Heapy Engineering LLP
Project Team: Joe Claude, Bart Grunenwald, Terry McKinney, Rod Rusnak, Matt Sciaretti, Rich Simpkins, Richard Weber, Tom Monnig

Cost Consultant: Cronenberg & Company Inc.
Principal: Dick Cronenberg

Civil: Infrastructure Services Inc.
Project Team: Maureen Parsons, Eric Batt

Code: Brashear-Bolton
Principal: Joe Brashear

Construction Manager: Messer Construction
Project Team: Ken Bloomer, Kurt Bouley, Steve Eder, Justin Koenes, Rick Schmithorst

Graphic/Wayfinding: Kolar Design with Marcia Shortt
Principals-in-Charge: Kelly Kolar, Marcia Shortt
Designers: Becky Ruehl, Donald Carson, David Eyman, Janice Radlove, TJ Schmidlin, Mary Dietrich

Furniture: Design Details Inc.
Project Team: Pam Irvin, NCIDQ, Ann Schrader

Photography: All images by Alan Karchmer except as noted:
Pages 26, 83, 90–91, 93, 94, 95, 101 photos by Ron Pollard
Page 97 photo by Andrew Higley/University of Cincinnati
Page 22 (bottom) and page 76 (bottom) photos by Moore Ruble Yudell

Sketches by Mario Violich
Additional drawings by Moore Ruble Yudell/glaserworks
Page 20 drawing by Kolar Design/Marcia Shortt

Selected Awards for Joseph A. Steger Student Life Center
2006 AIA National Honor Award
2005 AIA Ohio Merit Award
2005 AIA California Council Merit Award
2005 AIA Los Angeles Merit Award
2005 AIA Committee on Architecture for Education Merit Award
2004 AIA Cincinnati Honor Award for Collaboration

Selected Bibliography

Bach, John. (September, 2004). "Main Street al fresco." *University of Cincinnati Horizons, 34(1)*, p. 20–21.
Bach, John. (September, 2004). "Meet me on Main Street." *University of Cincinnati Horizons, 34(1)*, p. 14–15.
Bach, John. (September, 2004). "New facility sparks student life around the clock." *University of Cincinnati Horizons, 34(1)*, p. 18–19.
Downs, Maggie. (May 21, 2004). "UC's newest mainstay: A two-day celebration starting today will preview three Main Street projects." *Cincinnati Enquirer*, p. A1, A6.
Friedman, D.S. (Spring, 2005). "Campus design as critical practice: Notes on University of Cincinnati's new master plan." *Places, 17(1)*, p. 12–19.
Litt, Steven. (February, 2005). "UC x 3." *Metropolis, 24(6)*, p. 90–94, 106–107.
Merkel, Jayne. (April, 2005). "Image: Today's big man on campus." *Architectural Record Review*, p. 11.
Merkel, Jayne. (August, 2005). "Joseph A. Steger Student Life Center: Moore Ruble Yudell and glaserworks insert a long, dynamic structure into a tight site, binding a campus and community together." *Architectural Record, 193(8)*, p. 118–123.
Snoonian, Deborah. (August, 2005). "Meeting places." *Architectural Record, 193(8)*, p. 117.
Stephens, Suzanne. (February, 2000). "The American campus." *Architectural Record*, p. 77–79.

Buzz Yudell, FAIA, Partner

Buzz's passion for architecture grew out of a synthesis of artistic and social concerns. While at Yale College, his work in sculpture was complemented by his exploration of sciences and the humanities. Graduate studies at the Yale School of Architecture expanded these boundaries to a range of scales, from small construction in situ to community participation and urban design. Here, he began his long association with Charles Moore. In 1977, Buzz joined Charles and John Ruble in a partnership based on shared humanistic values and a celebration of collaboration within the office and beyond to their clients and communities.

Buzz has collaborated intensively with John to expand the firm's expression and expertise to include campus, cultural, civic, residential, and commercial architecture. Together, they have led the firm as pioneers in planning and architecture for sustainable communities. Working in Europe for over twenty-five years, Buzz and John bring advanced approaches to sustainable architecture to numerous projects in the United States.

Buzz has led project design on a broad array of community and civic projects, including the Joseph A. Steger Student Life Center at the University of Cincinnati; Manzanita Village Housing at the University of California, Santa Barbara; the Camana Bay Town Master Plan, Grand Cayman; master planning for new towns in Germany; master planning for housing and community facilities within the Santa Monica Civic Center Plan; sustainable urban housing for the Bo01 Housing Exhibition in Malmö, Sweden; the new Santa Monica Public Library; the new United States Embassy in Berlin, Germany; and master planning and new buildings for campuses including the University of California, Berkeley, the University of California, Los Angeles, Dartmouth College, Massachusetts Institute of Technology, and the California Institute of Technology.

Throughout his career, Buzz has found teaching, writing, and community service to be critical in the evolution of architecture's theoretical and cultural role in shaping and celebrating place and community. He has taught at Yale, UCLA, and the University of Texas, Austin. He was also honored with the distinguished Howard Friedman Chair of Architecture at the University of California, Berkeley. Together with John Ruble, Buzz received the 2007 American Institute of Architects (AIA) Los Angeles Gold Medal Award.

John Ruble, FAIA, Partner

John began his career as architect and planner in the Peace Corps, Tunisia, where a profound experience of culture, climate, and place provided lasting influences on his work. While working with Princeton, New Jersey architect Jules Gregory, he designed a series of award-winning public schools and civic projects before moving to California in the mid-seventies. At the University of California, Los Angeles, he studied and associated with Charles Moore, joining Charles and Buzz Yudell in partnership in 1977.

Since co-founding Moore Ruble Yudell, John Ruble has collaborated with his partners on a broad spectrum of residential, academic, cultural, and urban design work. As Partner-in-Charge, he has helped realize some of the firm's best-known international work, including the firm's competition-winning design for the United States Embassy in Berlin and the National AIA Honor Award-winning Comprehensive Master Plan for the University of Washington, Tacoma.

As Moore Ruble Yudell's portfolio has expanded into new areas of expertise—from laboratories to courthouses—John has sought to make each work part of a broad, sustained exploration in the creation of place. Current projects such as the South Lawn Project at the University of Virginia, the French Family Science Center at Duke University, and the recently completed U.S. Courthouse and Federal Building in Fresno continue to expand Moore Ruble Yudell's reputation and influence in civic architecture and urban development.

With architecture degrees from the University of Virginia and the University of California, Los Angeles School of Architecture and Urban Planning, John has been active in teaching and research, leading graduate design studios at UCLA and Cornell University. Together with Buzz Yudell, John is the 2007 AIA Los Angeles Gold Medal recipient.

Mario J. Violich, AIA, ASLA, Principal

With his background in landscape architecture and architecture, Mario Violich's professional and academic experiences blur the traditional boundaries between building and landscape. Mario received his Bachelor of Landscape Architecture degree at the University of California, Berkeley in 1983, followed by his Master of Architecture degree in 1989 from the University of California, Los Angeles. He joined Moore Ruble Yudell the same year.

Mario's design leadership has influenced a broad spectrum of projects at Moore Ruble Yudell, ranging from master planning, to mixed-use urban projects, to institutional buildings, to numerous single-family homes and gardens. His design approach is rooted in the exploration of the interdisciplinary nature of the design process. As featured in the design-process sketches in this publication, his drawings represent an ongoing exploration of new ways of imagining and representing the built environment in the early design phases.

As Principal-in-Charge, Mario's recent award-winning projects include the Joseph A. Steger Student Life Center at the University of Cincinnati, Ohio and the Beth El Synagogue in Berkeley, California. Additional recent work includes the NBCU Backlot Masterplan in Los Angeles, California; the National Tropical Botanical Gardens Library in Kauai, Hawaii; and the Law-Business Connection at the University of California, Berkeley. Mario's exploration of the relationship of landscape and building has evolved into the design of many single-family homes and gardens throughout California, including the Moir Residence in Monterey, the Livermore residence in Carmel, the Falkenberg Residence in Woodside, and the Schetter Residence in Pacific Palisades. He was also the principal designer on the recently completed Ruddell Residence in Kauai, Hawaii.

In addition to his broad, interdisciplinary professional experience, Mario has been an instructor in the Department of Landscape Architecture at UCLA Extension since 1993 and an associate teacher with Adjunct Professor Buzz Yudell at UCLA. He has been invited as a guest critic and lecturer to the Southern California Institute of Architecture, UC Berkeley's College of Environmental Design, and the University of Cincinnati's School of Architecture and Planning.

Adam A. Padua, Associate, Assoc. AIA, LEED® AP

Adam approaches architectural design with passion, patience, and interdisciplinary rigor. He graduated from the University of Chicago with a Bachelor's degree in Economics with general honors in 1979. He pursued a career designing systems software before coming to architecture. Adam first worked with Moore Ruble Yudell founder Charles Moore while at the University of California, Los Angeles, where he received a Master of Architecture degree in 1992. He joined Moore Ruble Yudell the same year.

He has a keen interest in shaping a built environment sensitive to its context—architecture integrated with inviting, open spaces and landscapes. He has managed complex campus, housing, and civic projects, including transformative renovation, new construction from programming through design and construction, design guidelines, and master planning. He has managed complicated projects involving multiple and, at times, multilingual client and user groups, agency reviews, and approvals.

His work as Project Manager includes the Horace Mann School in San Jose and the Joseph A. Steger Student Life Center at the University of Cincinnati, which garnered eleven design awards, including two National AIA Design Awards and two Education Facility Design Awards from the National AIA CAE. At the Steger Center, Adam took special pleasure in the breadth of design challenges, including the design of the zinc skin, atrium, and canopy, Mews Gardens landscape, specialty lighting, and wringing efficiencies from the 700-foot-long project.

Adam combines design sensitivity with skills in technical coordination. Throughout the design process, he works collaboratively with associate engineers and designers. As Senior Designer, his current projects include the United States Embassy, Berlin, Germany; a security upgrade of Pariser Platz, Berlin; the South Lawn Project Master Plan and academic buildings for the University of Virginia College of Arts and Sciences; and the American Institute in Taipei, Taiwan for the U.S. State Department.

Moore Ruble Yudell has earned a national and international reputation for excellence in design based on an unwavering commitment to humanistic principles and thoughtful development of unique solutions to an extraordinary range of projects and places. Under the leadership of Partners John Ruble and Buzz Yudell, and Principals Krista Becker, Jeanne Chen, Michael Martin, Neal Matsuno, James Mary O'Connor, and Mario Violich, the firm has built a diverse portfolio of award-winning work that embraces and addresses the critical concerns of community, identity, and place. Their personal interest in creating meaningful and memorable places that are inspired by climatic and cultural understanding has guided the firm's work at all scales: from individual houses, to academic and civic buildings, to master planning and the design of whole communities.

What initially began as a collaboration among the original partners has today expanded to include a broader community of public- and private-sector clients and colleagues, adding vitality and authenticity to the design process and ultimately enriching the quality and meaning of each work. The firm's work has been featured in numerous exhibitions and publications, and has been recognized with over 200 awards for design excellence, including the **2007 American Institute of Architects (AIA) Los Angeles Gold Medal** for John Ruble and Buzz Yudell, the **Royal Architectural Institute of Canada National Urban Design Award**, two **Chicago Athenaeum American Architecture Awards**, and seven **National AIA Honor Awards**. In 2006, Moore Ruble Yudell received the **AIA Architecture Firm Award**, the highest recognition the National American Institute of Architects can bestow.

In making this award, the AIA Committee on Design stated:

The firm has consistently produced an outstanding body of work rooted in a deep commitment to humanistic architecture. Their work is widely admired for its spirited celebration of habitation at many scales and its respect for people, context, and place. The firm continues to evolve in response to new challenges and opportunities while remaining true to the fundamental principles of humanism.

With an office of more than sixty multidisciplinary professionals, Moore Ruble Yudell has sustained a wide range of design efforts throughout the U.S. and around the globe. In addition to the partners and principals, the firm's leadership has evolved to include Senior Associates Stanley Anderson, director of the interior design group, and Bob Dolbinski. Each member of the leadership brings his or her own unique perspective and a diverse set of talents in leading project design and management, while enriching both the office culture and project development.

glaserworks' mission is to produce extraordinary buildings and memorable places. Its talented staff brings knowledge, experience, and genuine enthusiasm to the design process. It employs critical thinking, risk-taking, and the dispassionate evaluation of alternatives to help clients weigh the long-term consequences of key design decisions.

Now in its fiftieth year of practice, glaserworks continually improves the firm by making investments in its people, strategic alliances, processes for delivery, and knowledge base. Its most recent innovation is their three studios: Studio 3, Mixed-Use, and Culture & Higher Education. The first studio addresses issues that are important to the city; the other two address issues unique to developers and to institutions. Those clients whose projects engage all three studios will enjoy the creative dialogue among them.

glaserworks strives to assemble the right staff and the right consultant team for each project, while using its judgment to bring the right information to bear—at the right level and at the right time—to lead the team and the project to a successful conclusion.

glaserworks has earned a reputation for unswerving dedication to its clients' interests and also for maintaining gracious and supportive relationships with signature architects. The quality of the firm's work has been acknowledged in more than forty design awards received from local and state chapters of the American Institute of Architects, the National Association of Industrial and Office Parks, the Waterfront Association, and the Cincinnati Preservation Association.

ACKNOWLEDGEMENTS

We wish to thank Oscar Riera Ojeda and his colleagues at ORO *editions* for the opportunity to broaden and extend the unique story of the Joseph A. Steger Student Life Center at the University of Cincinnati. This project continues our ongoing collaboration beginning in 1997 with the publication of *Campus & Community*.

Writer Steven Litt has contributed his thoughtful and keen observations on the Steger Center. His broad perspective on the evolution of this building and its unique program and site context began in 2005 with his writing for *Metropolis* magazine. We are also grateful to Ron Kull for his essay. His unique perspective as the former campus architect beautifully highlights the specific qualities of the Steger Center site and the manner in which it influenced the programmatic composition and shaping of the building.

Matt Kanaracus of Codesign, in collaboration with Oscar Riera Ojeda, established the graphic-design framework for this publication. Ken Kim, our own editor for design and production, has made countless contributions both to the content and quality of this publication with assistance from James Mary O'Connor, Adam Padua, Karou Orime, Philippe Arias, Van Chu, and Takuji Mukaiyama.

Any presentation of built works depends largely on photography. In this case, the project unfolds through multiple still images documenting movement and habitation. We have had the fortune of telling this story of building and choreography through the extraordinary eye of Alan Karchmer. We are also grateful to photographer Ron Pollard and the University of Cincinnati for providing additional key images.

The Steger Center was an exceptional challenge and a wonderful experience for all of us who worked together on its design and realization, from campus planners to university administrators, students, and collaborating designers. Our building was rooted in the shared and inspired vision of the University of Cincinnati under the leadership of Joseph Steger, Ron Kull, Dale McGirr, and the Design Review Board. Their combined efforts were realized by an inspired and thoughtful master plan by Hargreaves and Associates. Our collaboration with Morphosis and Gwathmey Siegel was creatively and collegially gratifying, guided and nurtured by the university. Ultimately, our success was rooted in the extraordinary contributions from our local associate firm, glaserworks.

Finally, we wish to acknowledge the administrators, students, and teachers of the University of Cincinnati. They are and will continue to be a key inspirational force behind this project and our current and future university work.

—John Ruble, Buzz Yudell, and Mario Violich

ORO *editions*
Publishers of Architecture, Art, and Design
Gordon Goff & Oscar Riera Ojeda – Publishers
West Coast: PO Box 150338, San Rafael, CA 94915
East Coast: 143 South Second Street, Ste. 208, Philadelphia, PA 19106
www.oroeditions.com
info@oroeditions.com

Copyright © 2008 by ORO *editions*

ISBN: 978-0-9795395-0-3

Series Concept: Oscar Riera Ojeda (oscar@oroeditions.com)
Graphic Design: Matt Kanaracus, Codesign (matt@codesignco.com) and Oscar Riera Ojeda
Project Coordination: Ken Kim (kkim@mryarchitects.com), Jill Tabler-Koperweis (jill@oroeditions.com), and Matt Kanaracus
Copy Edits: Nirmala Nataraj (nirmala@nirmalanataraj.com)
Foreign-Edition Sales: Gordon Goff (gordon@oroeditions.com)
Production: Joanne Tan-Ling (joanne@oroeditions.com), Oscar Riera Ojeda, and Gordon Goff
Color Separation and Printing: ORO *editions* HK
Covers: Toyo Saifu cloth custom dyed in Japan
End Paper Sheets: 140 gsm wood-free from NPI, Tokyo
Text Paper: 150 gsm Tri-pine matte; an off-line gloss spot varnish was applied to all photographs
Fonts: Trade Gothic and Trade Gothic Condensed

Printed in China by ORO *editions* HK

Distribution

In North America:
Distributed Art Publishers, Inc.
155 Sixth Avenue, Second Floor
New York, NY 10013
USA

In Europe:
RIBA Bookshops
15 Bonhill Street
London, EC2P 2EA
United Kingdom

In Asia:
Page One Publishing Private Ltd.
20 Kaki Bukit View
Kaki Bukit Techpark II, 415967
Singapore